To
Chuck!

BIKER TO SAILOR

The True Story of Bob Bitchin

Get outta Bed & Let's Go out on a Boat!

Bob B.

Book & Cover Design: Bob Bitchin
Cover Art: Richard "Magic" Marker
Editor: Sue Morgan

This book is non-fiction except for where a 70+ year memory failed the author, probably from the use of drugs at an early age. That said, it is as close to the way it was remembered as possible. The names & places are mostly accurate, however, when a bumbling memory would not bring forth factual names or locations the author filled these in from his very fertile imagination. Any resemblances to actual events, locations or persons, living or dead or even semi-live was as it was meant to be.

ISBN: 978-0-9662182-7-5 (Print)
ISBN: 978-0-9662182-8-2 (Digital)

Submit all requests for reprinting to:
FTW Publishing
Box 100
Berry Creek, CA 95916

Published in the United States by FTW Publishing, Inc.

www.bobbitchin.com
www.seafaring.com
www.TheBitchinGroup.com

First Printing - August 2015

Dedicated to my wife Jody
*Only God knows how much she has had to
endure just to keep my juices flowing!*

Other Books By Bob Bitchin

Non Fiction
Biker

True accounts of the outlaw motorcycle culture in the 70's & 80's in the United States and Europe. These are true adventures of what the motorcycling brotherhood was all about.

Letters from The Lost Soul

A 5 year voyage of discovery that takes the reader on a real-life adventure aboard the SV Lost Soul. This is the book that created Latitudes & Attitudes TV and Cruising Outpost Magazine.

The Sailing Life

A look at what makes the sailing life such an adventure, and gives an insight into what can be learned by casting off the dock-lines.

Starboard Attitude

Similar to the popular book "The Sailing Life" this book takes you into the mind of what makes sailors do the things we do. Insights into what it means to cross an ocean.

Fiction
A Brotherhood of Outlaws

A Treb Lincoln novel that follows a group of outlaws thru a myriad of adventures riding around the country and organizing a protest against the governments interference with their freedom.

Emerald Bay

Follow Treb Lincoln on an adventure which starts when a drug lord boat explodes in Emerald Bay, and the trail leads Treb and his friends all the way to Central America and the CIA.

King Harbor

Treb Lincoln returns to his boat in King Harbor, and before long he is involved in a race across the Pacific to try and save the lives of hundreds of islanders, and the wife of a close friend.

These books available at www.bobbitchin.com and Amazon

BIKER TO SAILOR

The true 35 year odyssey that took a man from the most
violent and drug-crazed segment of society to the
quietest and most mellow lifestyle on earth.

By Bob Btchin

Berry Creek, California

Blending in Is Not An Option
By Sue Morgan - Editor

The mid '70s through the '80s were a unique time in King Harbor, Redondo Beach, CA. Boating in general was at a peak and there was a long waiting list for slips. There was a huge liveaboard community both in the marinas and at the mooring field in the outer harbor. Everybody pretty much knew everyone and it was a very social lifestyle.

The liveaboard community crossed every demographic and you became friends with people you'd probably never meet if it wasn't for the common denominator of boating. Old, young and everything in between, doctors, lawyers, engineers, construction workers, mechanics, secretaries (remember those?) all hung out together.

No one really cared about what you did; it was all about boats and life aboard. Once we shed our business attire and we were in our boat clothes we were all the same. Everyone blended in. Almost...

Bob Bitchin did not blend, nor did he make any attempt to. His sheer size made him stand out, but he was also obviously a biker. A rather scary, I think I'll cross the street to avoid making contact looking biker, with more tattoos than I'd ever seen before. He dressed all in black and wore some very menacing looking jewelry with spikes that would take your eye out. We didn't know what he did for a living and weren't sure we wanted to. Needless to say, he did not look like a boater, let alone a sailor.

We got to know him when our friend, Guy Spencer, bought Bob's boat Outlaw. Bob had just bought the first Lost Soul and was already planning to go cruising, as were many of us. He became one of the liveaboard community and hung out with the rest of us talking boats, cruising equipment, provisioning, etc. Despite appearances he was friendly, funny, smart, and he really was a sailor. He was one of us.

All of us liked to cruise over to Catalina Island and we frequently ran into Bob over there on Lost Soul. On one occasion a lot of us were anchored in Cat Harbor on the back side of the Isthmus to celebrate the New Year. On New Year's morning my husband Mike and I were taking an early morning dinghy/coffee cruise. Bob saw us and waved us aboard. After some chit chat Bob decided we needed some music and went below to turn on the stereo. Soon, at quite a high volume, some odd but strangely familiar noises started coming from the on-deck speakers. Moans, groans and heavy breathing had heads popping out of hatches around the anchorage. Then hatches started slamming shut. Instead of turning on the music Bob had turned on a sound recording that he'd made with two people loudly making love. Half of me wanted to hide and the other half was laughing too hard to move. Blend in? Nope.

For many different reasons, by the end of the '80s life in King Harbor was changing a lot. There were restrictions on the number of liveaboards and lots of people moved on to a more "normal" lifestyle. Some of us have hung in there and some new people have joined our ranks. It's still a great way to live because for those of us here, regardless of what we do (or don't do) for a living, we're all boaters. We all blend in.

I've known Bob a whole lotta years now and I have to say he has mellowed a lot. The biker black has been slowly replaced with Hawaiian shirts. Biker boots evolved into sandals. Appearance-wise, he can sort of pass as a boater these days, and the crazy shenanigans (there have been many I was witness to) are a little less "in your face." But blend in? No way. Thank goodness!

Sue Morgan and her husband Mike have lived aboard their Cheoy Lee yawl "Beacause" for over 35 years. She is the editor of this book, and has been editor of Latitudes & Attitudes & Cruising Outpost Magazines for the past 17 years.

Biker to Sailor
The True Story of Bob Bitchin

› Chapter 1 ‹
Attitude

It was a blustery day, blowing about 55 knots in the Alinuihaha Channel between the Big Island of Hawaii and Maui. The seas were running about 30 feet, but we were running downwind and at an angle to the swells, so it wasn't too bad. We had a triple-reefed main and just a handkerchief of a headsail out, but we were still managing a respectable 8-8.5 knots. I was at the helm because the autopilot, "Fred," just couldn't handle it when we slid down a wave face.

All of a sudden I noticed the boat sat upright and the headsail started flogging. "That's odd," I thought. "Why would my headsail be flogging with this much wind? The only thing that could cause that would be…"

And as I looked around and back over my shoulder, I saw what had blocked the wind. It was an 80-foot wall of water! I knew it was at least 80 feet since my mast was 74 feet, and it was well over that. And as luck would have it, the very top

1

was crystal clear.

Okay, now anyone in the class have an idea why this is a bad thing?

Yup, you got it. Clear at the top means the wave is about to break!

So here I am, standing at the wheel of my 42-ton, 68-foot ketch, Lost Soul, without a harness on (okay, we'll get to that later!) and I am about to have an 80-foot wall of water come crashing down on me. It was a rogue wave. That's where two large waves running in slightly different directions cross. It was two 30-foot waves crossing, which made about a 50-foot wave. But when measuring a wave you need to include the distance into the "valley" between the two waves. We were in said valley!

As the wave started to pass beneath us the boat did what it was supposed to do. It floated up the face. However, there was a small problem. As we were quartering the wave the starboard side had less water under it than the port side. This caused the boat to roll to starboard. As we drifted up the face of the wave the boat started to heel at a pretty steep angle. And then we were high enough on the wave for the wind to catch the sails. Fifty-five knots of wind in the sails heeled us even more.

I wrapped my arm thru the 42-inch wooden-spoked wheel at the helm and locked my arms tight. As we reached the top of the wave the boat had rolled to about 45°... and then the wave broke. The mast went past the 90° angle. The deck was past being vertical to the sea and I was kinda hanging in mid air from the ship's wheel.

This was about where I decided perhaps my rule aboard Lost Soul might need re-writing. My rule was that in bad weather everyone but the skipper had to don a safety harness. From this point on the rule would be re-thought!

As the wave broke over us the water curled over the boat leaving an air pocket where I was hanging. I remember looking over to see that Jody was safe. She had been sitting in the enclosed storm room on the starboard side. When I glanced over in her direction she was laying on her back against the window of the storm room, still in her seat. In a situation like that things move at a much slower pace in your mind. I remember thinking how kewl it was being dry with a wall of water washing over the boat.

When we were first blanketed by the wave I figured we were doing about 8.5 knots. As we slid down the face of the huge wave we probably sped up to around 9-9.5 knots. Now I am no physicist, but I do know you don't just stop 42 tons of mass moving at 9 knots. So what happened next was not surprising. The mast kind of augered into the water, and then the physics of a mono-hull with 20,000 pounds of weight hanging from her bottom took over. The boat righted herself. Once again, it seemed to be in slow motion. As the boat "flipped" to the upright position, I was pulled back onto my feet and once again I was looking forward thru the dodger. The triple-reefed main was full of water.

Now I don't know if I mentioned this, but it was a brilliantly sunny day. As I watched it looked like Niagara Falls was falling on my deck out of the mainsail. I looked down to where Jody was sitting (she was right back where she had been sitting when it all stated), and said, "Jody, you gotta see this, it's beautiful!"

She was just sitting there with a stunned look on her face, like I was some sort of an idiot speaking Greek. It was at this point in our cruising life that I came up with the saying, "Attitude is the difference between ordeal and adventure."

And it was also at this point where Jody came up with the saying, "Sometimes it's just an ordeal!"

> Chapter 2 <
What Kinda Nut Does This?

Sailing long distances across oceans is not the brightest of ideas. I mean, look at what it is we do "for fun." We spend copious amounts of hard-earned money to buy a boat. Said boat is usually slightly larger than a jail cell. Then we board said boat and sail off into the most inhospitable place on earth - the ocean; a place filled with water you can't drink, things that eat you, and occasionally waves that are taller then three- to five-story buildings. Once we are out there we pull up a couple of bed sheets and think that we will actually see land at the end of our voyage.

We gotta be nuts!

But ya know what? After about 40 years of doing it, I can't imagine not doing it.

So now that we've looked at the futility of what we do, let's take a look at the reality. There is no other lifestyle like sailing.

Picture this: You have been fighting a gale for the past few hours. It came on you about two a.m. For some reason that's when they like to hit, but that's another story. Your boat is ready for bad weather and as the squall passes over, you stand at the wheel and feel as if you are pushing the boat thru it. But now, as you look to the horizon, you start to see a little light under the dark storm clouds. The seas start to subside and soon you are shaking the reef out of the sails and you are once again sailing across a beautiful blue sea. Off in the distance you see Bora Bora, the most beautiful island in the world.

Living that adventure fills you with joy; the joy of accomplishing something! You can't get it reading a book (like this one). No, you have to get out there and fight the dragon in order to kiss the princess. You have to fight the good fight to feel the joy of winning. The more hard fought a crossing, the more heartfelt the joy!

The vast majority of our friends and relatives think we are a few French fries short of a Happy Meal. There is no way they can conceive of a reason to do such a thing. And to us, there is no way we could think of living and NOT doing it. For them there is no explanation. For us, none is needed.

In the following pages (or, in this day and age, probably on your favorite electronic reading gadget!), I will endeavor to give you a glimpse into one man's journey from being a land-dwelling slug to a "seasoned" sailor. First I have an admission to make. I was not one of those "born to sail" people who talk about being raised from a tadpole on a boat. In fact, the first time I went sailing I was over 30 years old. It was more by accident than by design, and I am living proof that any fool can learn to sail.

> Chapter 3 <
My Introduction to Sailing 101

I became a sailor more out of spite than anything else. You see, "back in the day," being a sailor was about the last thing in the world I ever thought I'd be. By the time I'd turned 30 I had been thru my stint serving my country as a fly-boy in the Air Force. I had been married at 18, had my first child before I was 19 and my second before I was 21. I'd been divorced, lived as a hippie in

Bob in the early seventies. Not your "born sailor" type.

8

Venice Beach (California) and had already started a couple of small businesses including a carpet store, a head shop (c'mon, you remember those, right?), a gym, a martial arts equipment retail store and a travel agency. But my main purpose in life was devoted to the worship of the two-wheeled beast known as a Harley-Davidson.

One night I met this nut while riding my true love down Sunset Boulevard in Hollywood. He was wearing a fur coat and driving a convertible Maserati. We stopped at a light and he was looking over my bike, while I was looking over his car. The light changed and we both wicked it on full throttle.

I hate to admit this, but he kicked my ass! I had him for the first half-block, and then it was all about horsepower. He turned into the parking lot at Cyrano's (an eatery where I could never afford to eat), and as he pulled in he flagged me over.

Okay now, I gotta tell ya. I was tossed. Here's this dude wearing a fur coat asking me to pull over, so I'm thinking, this being Hollywood and such... well, you know. But at the same time, a Maserati convertible is not something you see every day, and I'd never even seen one as a convertible. My mind was made up when I saw his license plate. It was from Montana and just had the word "Evel."

Long story short, that night Evel and I had a little too much fun. By 5:00 in the morning I was being locked up in the West Hollywood Police

Station with a dude named Filthy McNasty. Filthy (yes, that is his legal name!), owned the nightclub we'd been partying at. It seems the Bureau of Alcohol, Tobacco and Firearms (ATF) had a rule about serving booze after 2:00 a.m. in a bar. At two the doors had been closed, but the booze kept flowing.

The following evening I was being interviewed by a guy from Rolling Stone who was doing an article on Evel and the coming jump at the L.A. Coliseum. He was asking about the previous evening's adventure which included, but was not limited to, Evel Knievel, me, Wolfman Jack (the Disc Jockey), and a group of strippers from the Classic Cat burlesque house which was right next door to Filthy McNasty's. Oh, and Filthy's was across the street and a half block down from the Whiskey-a-Go-Go. It was the old Melody Room, which was infamous in the '50s and '60s and later became the Viper Room where River Phoenix died.

So, what, you are asking yourself, does this have to do with sailing, right? It's just to show you that, as I have said, any idiot can sail. Read on.

Okay, so by the end of the week I was hanging out with Knievel helping him get ready for his jump at the L.A. Coliseum. It was fun, to say the least, hanging out with this guy. I became his bodyguard and party partner after he asked his pilot to help stop him at the top of the ramp he'd set up for the jump, and the pilot refused saying

Bob (on left) with Knievel & Mike Draper

you'd have to be crazy to stand in front of Knievel coming up the ramp at 60 mph. At the top of the ramp were two 4x8 sheets of plywood where he had to stop and turn the bike around.

Knievel looked at him and said, "You're fired. Get out of here." Then he turned to me.

"Would you catch me?" Hell yeah! I thought. What a gas!

For the next few weeks we hung out, partying every night. I got to meet a lot of real celebrities and it ended up changing my life.

After the jump I worked with him setting up the Snake River Canyon jump, and once that was over I moved on. With the connections I'd made

Knievel holding up his cover on Biker News to cover Bob's face.

with Evel I soon started Biker News, a tabloid all about the outlaw motorcycle life in Southern California.

So now we are going to get into my actual introduction to sailing.

One day my editor, Degenerate Jim, and I hopped on our bikes to go to lunch. We'd planned on going to Momma Rosa's for burritos and beer, but it was packed so we rode down to King Harbor in Redondo Beach, about a mile away, and went to Captain Ahab's. They had hotter waitresses anyway! After lunch, as we were leaving the restaurant, I heard a banging on one of the docks. I looked over and there was a guy putting a "For Sale" sign on a boat.

Now, here I must digress. You see, me and my partner in the head shop I owned, "Hermosa High," had used some perks from my travel agency for a little flight to Tahiti a month or two before this. We'd stayed at the Club Med in Moorea. Back in the good old days, Club Med was for singles only. Well, while we were there, it turned out that there were two women to every man, and most of them were from Australia. This, at the time, was quite an advantage for American males. In fact, it was better than walking thru a women's prison with a pocket full of pardons, if you get my drift.

So, at the end of our stay, the folks at Club Med offered us a chance to stay on to help the ladies have a good time, as jogging instructors (???!). It would have been a dream come true, but alas, I had responsibilities and deadlines. My partner Patrick had no such claims on his time, so he stayed in Tahiti and I flew home.

About a month later I got a call from Patrick. He'd met a couple guys on a yacht anchored off the beach at Club Med and they'd offered him a chance to sail from Tahiti to Hawaii. Okay, so I was so green with envy I probably glowed.

And then I found myself standing in King Harbor Marina watching a boat go up for sale.

"Hey, dude!" I hollered across the water. "What's the deal on the boat?"

He stood staring at us for about a minute. We must have made an odd picture there at this beautiful marina. Degenerate Jim looked like a cross between the dude in ZZ Top and Charles Manson. He was wearing a cut-off Levi jacket with patches from various motorcycle events, dark glasses that he never removed, a beard that reached down to his belly button and big, black motorcycle boots.

I, on the other hand, was what I considered at the time to be dressed appropriately. Standing about 6'4" and weighing in at about 285, I had been pumping iron at the gym I owned, "Grunt & Sweat Gym," so was just wearing a T-shirt with the sleeves cut off and my Levis cutoff with a big patch on the back saying "Biker News" and a rocker at the bottom saying "So Cal." I was still wearing my "rings" I had when I was Knievel's bodyguard. That is a very large silver ring on every finger, mostly skulls and large daemon heads. Of course, both of us were sporting tattoos as I was, at the time, just starting Tattoo Magazine.

He opened the gate hesitantly and we walked down to the boat. Now, you have to try and imagine what people on the dock were thinking. Kinda like having a center seat on an airplane and then seeing a couple of Sumo wrestlers walking to your row to sit down.

14

So, we are going to make this long story short. I bought the boat, a Cal 28 with a 9hp outboard on the back. I asked the seller to give me five sailing lessons if I bought it, but he said he could only give me three because he was leaving for Hawaii that Friday on the 50-foot ketch at the end of the dock.

> Chapter 4 <
Day One, or, Losing My Virginity

I have to admit I was more than a little nervous. After pulling off my boots, I boarded the boat and when I stepped on it the whole boat started to sink on the side I was boarding, or at least that's what it felt like. I jumped back onto the dock and looked at the seller with an "are you sure about this" look in my eye.

"Don't worry," he said. "Once you're amidships the boat will right itself."

I understood the words, "Don't worry," but the rest of what he said could have been in Greek. But not wanting him to think I was afraid (you know, manly men on manly ships, right?) I stepped on again and quickly stepped down into the cockpit. He was right. All was well once I was standing there.

Meanwhile, he was dashing all over the boat doing God only knows what. I watched and wondered if I would ever understand what he was doing, and wondered even more, what the hell had

I gotten myself into!

He lifted the center area of the back bench where the outboard was located, and pulled on the starter cord. It fired right up. "Kewl!" I thought. I can do that!

Then he jumped off the boat and started untying the dock lines. "You are coming with me, right?" I asked timidly.

"Oh yeah, just gotta cast off the dock lines."

Ahh. More lingo to learn. Cast off obviously meant to leave somewhere, and dock lines, even I could understand that. Maybe this wasn't going to be too bad after all.

As we motored up the channel he started pulling on one of the many ropes that were laying around and the big sail in the middle of the boat started to rise.

"This is the halyard," he explained. "It raises the sail. This is the mainsail."

Yeah, right, I thought. Now I am supposed to remember the names of all these ropes. Like that's going to happen!

Okay, so far not too bad. This I could do, and I understood all of the magic behind it.

At the end of the channel he pulled on the stick that controlled the steering and the boat swung the other way. This seemed kind of odd, but I kept watching as he started to pull on another rope and a floppy sail started to rise from the pointy end of the boat. It flogged and made all kinds of noise, and just when I figured something

17

was really wrong and was about to swim back to shore, the boat started to fall over.

No, really! The whole boat started to roll over as the sail caught the wind. I grasped this big chrome thing with my arm and hung on for dear life! That, I later learned, was called a winch. The boat was leaning over at a 25° tilt at least!

"Hey," he said in a deceptively calm voice, "would you mind easing the sheet a little bit?"

I just stared at him as if he was crazy. Why would I want to go and grab a sheet? Who could sleep in this death-trap?

"The sheet is the line over there on the cleat," he said, pointing to what I assumed was a cleat. "Just un-cleat it and let it slip a little."

I sat there hanging onto my new best friend, the chrome thingy, and stared at him. Then I sat and watched how this seemingly normal individual wrapped a little line around the wood steery thingy (the tiller) and walked across the deck of the boat while it was heeled over so far I was sure we were going to flip over. As he let the line slip a little from the cleat, the boat came back to an almost normal slant, and once again, all was well with the world.

For the next two days at about 2:00 p.m. I would ride down to the marina and get a "lesson." I refused to try and learn what a halyard or sheet was, but became acquainted with the winches (my former best friend), cleats and tiller. By the end of day three I was hauling up the mainsail, trimming the headsail and starting to get the hang of pulling the tiller one way to go the other.

And then he was gone.

The next day I grabbed Degenerate Jim away from the typewriter and told him we were going sailing. We jumped on our bikes and headed down to the marina. I don't mind telling you I was more than a little worried, but excited as well.

We boarded Rogue, which was the name I'd given her, and I got the sails ready to raise. We released the dock lines and just as I started to push her out into the channel I realized I'd forgotten to start the outboard. Oops.

As we drifted towards the boats behind us I popped up the center seat, pulled the choke and gave it a pull. Thank God, it started. I don't even think Jim noticed how panicky I was.

As we motored into the wind I pulled the mainsail up and made the turn at the end of the channel. As I pulled the headsail up I noticed Jim start to grab my friend the winch, and when the wind caught it, well, his normal calm demeanor fell apart and he was hanging onto it for dear life. Inwardly I smiled. Three days earlier that had been me!

For the next few months, every day at the office I would pull Jim away from his desk and say, "Let's go sailing." We were both starting to really enjoy it. Every day we would head out of the marina and then sail about three miles north to where the oil tankers would moor to unload at the refinery. There, they had these huge mooring buoys. They had to be 35-40 feet long and about 10 feet in diameter. On top there was a cleat for the oil tankers to tie to. I would use the buoys to practice pulling along side. I didn't want to do it in the marina because if (when) I screwed up, I didn't want people laughing at me. After a couple weeks we got pretty good at it.

I was oblivious to what we must have looked like to the other boaters back then. I mean, there were times, like on a weekend, when two or three of my club brothers would ride down with their ol' ladies and six or eight of us would jump on Rogue and go out for a day sail. As we'd head out of the marina, all the men would be wearing Levis with black T-shirts, in most cases with something rude printed on them, motorcycle boots (yes, we wore them on the boat!) and sunglasses. The ladies, on

Learning how to sail on Rogue, a Cal 28.

the other hand, would usually be wearing panties and bras as we left the dock, and then would lose those as we'd turn the channel...

Which was right in front of the King Harbor Yacht Club. And I wondered years later, when I was sponsored for membership, why I was blackballed?

This was my intro to sailing. Who knew how it would change my life!

> Chapter 5 <
A Life-Changing Event

The phone rang. I was covering the evening shift at Hermosa High (our head shop). It was Patrick. He had sailed to Hawaii on a schooner with the guys he'd met at the Club Med in Moorea, and now he was calling from San Francisco. He had just sailed in on a 74-foot square-rigged topsail schooner, Stone Witch. It was the flagship for Greenpeace.

"Okay, listen," he said excitedly, "we have a chance to have a real adventure!"

He and I had been friends for a long time, and he knew that the word adventure would get me. He was right. For a moment I forgot how jealous I was of his recent adventure sailing across the Pacific, and bit the hook like a starving grouper downing a wayward sardine.

"Why, what's up?" I asked as I swallowed the hook, line and sinker.

"The guy who built the boat I just sailed in on wants to sail down to Guatemala. Problem is, he hasn't got the money to supply the ship for that kind of a voyage. He figures it would be a three-month voyage, and he'd need at least six-seven crew."

I had been sailing Rogue every day for three months and felt I was a real sailor by now. The thought of a three-month voyage down the Pacific Coast sounded like a dream.

"How much does he need to get ready? And if we do this, I have to figure out how to cover my ass with the magazine and here at the head shop."

"He said he'd need about $8,000, and for that we could take four-six people. I figured we could charge a couple grand for each, and all we'd need is four people to pay our way!"

Once again, to make a long story short (I keep saying that, but very seldom live up to it, have you noticed?), I told him to let me give it some thought and to call me the same time the next day. Well, to be honest with you (I know, why start now?), I had pretty much made up my mind I was going. But I had a few "little things" I had to sort out. First and foremost there was Patty, the girl I was living with at the time. We'd been together about a year and we were pretty happy. But then again, one of the things that kept us happy was that I kept coming up with little adventures. Like riding to Daytona Beach, Florida, from Redondo Beach, California, on my chopped Harley. Or sailing over to Catalina Island on the boat. She loved adventure almost more than I did.

As it turned out, that would be the least of my problems. She was all over it before I finished explaining what the whole deal was. Then again, she didn't have to figure out how to pay for all this. When Patrick said we could take four-five friends and they could pay a couple grand each, I knew he was dreaming. If you took all of our friends and emptied all of the piggy banks, I doubt if we would have had $800, much less $8,000.

And then there was my "day job." The reason I had the head shop and travel agency was because I had my job with the magazine to cover any losses, which, at times, were substantial. But I liked to travel, and I liked to do the occasional recreational drug. So it was worth it to me.

I discussed it with Degenerate Jim the next morning and he said to go for it. He could handle the magazine for three issues. He'd been working with me for a few years by then, and he was getting pretty tired of me dragging him out to the boat every day. He didn't see sailing as an adventure. More of an ordeal, you might say.

So, two down and one to go: how to get the money? And that, as it turned out, was the easiest part.

My fiend Kenny Condom (that was a nickname, honest!), was always saying how much he liked the boat I had and really wanted to get one. I had paid $10,000 for the boat when I bought it. I bought it for cash, which I had from a recent business transaction which I can't discuss here.

Not sure about the statute of limitations, if you get my drift! But anyway, I called Kenny and we made a deal. He'd give me $8,000 that he was going to get from selling his car, and then pay me the $2,000 when (if?) I got back.

And so it was, a month later Stone Witch came sailing into the harbor. Okay, now here, once again, I must digress. I was a newbie sailor and King Harbor, in Redondo Beach, is purely a small-craft harbor. At the time the biggest boat in our marina was about 50 feet. There were a couple 60-foot powerboats over by the Yacht Club, but nothing that could even start to compare with Stone Witch. When she sailed in she had her topsail furled, and came drifting in with just her main and headsail. You see, she didn't have a motor. She used four 21-foot sweeps (that means oars in salty talk) to maneuver. Her hull was black, her spars were wood, and her running lights were kerosene. She was, without any doubt, the most "salty" boat I had ever seen.

Over the next few days all of our friends came out to see this vessel we were going to "sail off into the sunset" on. Now keep in mind... this was about 1979. Most cruisers sailed boats between 27 and 35 feet. To me this was not a boat. It was more of a ship. In my opinion boats carry people and ships carry boats. On the foredeck sat a couple of tenders.

As it turned out, we could only find one friend who could come up with any money to join us. Patrick owed English Paul $500 which he "forgave," and then we handed Captain Alan Olsen $8,000.00 from the sale of my boat!

The crew for this voyage would be the Captain, Alan, who also built the boat from scratch, plus two crew who had helped him sail down from San Francisco. The first crewman was Woody Le Mar (not to be confused with Woody Henderson, who would sail with me almost 20 years later). Woody Le Mar was, in all ways, a man of the sea. He lived to sail and loved the life more than most. He always had a big grin on his face and was the first up the mast, the first to be ready to haul in the anchor, and was the First Mate. The other who sailed down was Dan Shugrue. Dan was young (21), well built, and was as eager as anyone I have met before or since to live and learn the sailing lifestyle. As a matter of fact, Dan is still "working" with Alan, helping build the new 132-foot tall ship being built by the Educational Tall Ship Foundation, of which Alan is the CEO.

The crew was rounded out by Patrick, English Paul, Patty and me. Patrick had been my partner in our little head shop before casting off from Tahiti and getting the sailing bug. His resemblance to Jesus Christ was uncanny, at least the images of that time. He was well built, about 6'1" with long brown hair, blue eyes, beard and mustache. English Paul was a dead-ringer for Eddy Van Halen with long blonde hair, blue eyes, a suave

English accent, and a list of about 20 girls' names tattooed down his left arm, each one crossed out when a new one was added. The last three names were Melissa, crossed out twice, but still legible at the bottom of the list. The only woman on the boat was really more of a girl. She had been riding with me for awhile and had just turned 18. She resembled Little Annie Fanny from Playboy (for those of you old enough to remember her) and was extremely well endowed with blonde hair, bright blue eyes, and a penchant for wearing the tightest Levis and Danskin tops she could find. And she had a smile that could light up a room.

This was a pretty motley crew (and this was

Bob with daughter Sabra on the left and Patty on the right

before Motley Crew was a musical group!); six scurvy-looking men and one 18-year-old girl. Of the whole crew only Alan, Dan and Patty didn't have tattoos. The rest of us stood over 6 feet and were a pretty rough looking bunch.

The last night in port we had a party on deck. Stone Witch had to stay anchored in the harbor because there were no slips big enough for her. So people came by dinghy out to the boat where a small generator had been set up to power the guitars and amps for the band. The band, by the way, was "The Guitars" and Casey, the lead singer, lived with Daniel, the bass player, and they ended up being my partners in the head shop for the next 35 years!

Anyway, it was an unforgettable night. The music was blasting across the harbor, and when the band would stop playing there was applause coming from the Portofino Hotel which was just above the breakwater. Oh, yeah, to round this all out a little, 25 years later when I came back from our world cruise and started Latitudes & Attitudes Magazine, our office was at the Portofino Hotel for as long as we published! It was also where I lived on my boat, and where I had met the woman who would ultimately become Mrs. Bitchin! But once again, I digress.

The morning after the night before was, well, lets say "not as jovial" as the party. There were a few bodies that had to be taken ashore. People were found sleeping in the anchor locker, spare bunks, and elsewhere. It was also one of those times when "sailors" didn't set off on a voyage. It was 13:13 hours on Friday the 13th. Many warned us it was a bad omen to leave. Yeah, right! Like we believed in omens!

It was time to lift the sails. This was the defining moment in my life. At that moment life changed. I was a boater.

We hauled the anchor by hand, and once it was stowed I watched as Alan (no one called him Al) magically maneuvered this behemoth out the mouth of the harbor. I got my first lesson in why it was so important to know the names of the lines. Because, if you didn't know the names (like me at the time), you stood there like a lump on a log watching everyone else do stuff.

"Haul the mainsail halyard!" Alan would holler and someone would grab one of the lines and start pulling on it. As it neared the top someone who actually knew what they were doing would join in, and as it neared the top they wrapped the line once around the bottom of a cleat on the base of the mast and "worried" it tight by keeping tension on the line around the cleat and pulling it tighter like a string on a guitar.

"Haul the staysail halyard and bring her amidships," said Alan, and I watched in awe as Dave, Woody and Patrick ran to another line. This one came down from the top of the mast and was tied to a belaying pin on the pin rail mounted between the fore and aft shroud.

Alan seemed to sense how I felt: stupid and useless. He glanced over at me for a second and as the boat turned out of the mouth of the harbor he said, "Don't worry, you'll get the hang of it soon enough."

> Chapter 6 <
I Just Want to Die

As we sailed out of the harbor and made a course for the tip of Palos Verdes Peninsula I was excited. We were on our way! Nothing could stop us now.

Palos Verdes Point was only about three miles away. But the closer we got the less wind we had. Soon it seemed as if we were standing still and the sea was like glass. Those who sailed in the area often called it the Palos Verdes Doldrums. It didn't seem to bother Alan. He just sat back with one hand on the tiller (yes, the huge ship used a tiller!) and relaxed.

The world stopped. All of a sudden we were sitting about a mile off one of the most populated areas in the U.S., but we might as well have been mid-ocean. It was quiet. You could see cars, but it was silent. We drifted with the current, and somehow Alan kept the boat "pointed" in the right direction. It didn't seem like there was any wind at all.

"Okay, let's open the main topsail and see if we can't catch some of the offshore breeze this afternoon," Alan said, to no one in particular.

The crew once again jumped to action, but this time they started climbing the rigging on little pieces of rope that were tied between the shrouds, which I later learned were called ratlins. Not hard to figure where that came from, as it literally was a shortened version of ratlines. Were they nuts? Once they got to the top they got onto a line that

SV Stone Witch

ran from one end of the topsail yard to the other. Standing only on this little 3/8" piece of rickety line called a foot rope, they spread out and untied the sail, and as they did it dropped.

I stood there stunned. On the huge topsail that had just opened there was painted a full-sized humpback whale. All of a sudden it came back to me. This is the flagship for Greenpeace. It was a new organization at that time, but it had been on the news plenty, and here I was about to sail on the flagship for Greenpeace all the way to Guatemala.

On deck Patrick undid one of the lines on the pin rail and pulled it tight, tightening the topsail. He looked at Alan, who said "Ease it a little, a little more. Good. Secure." Dan then repeated it on the other side of the boat. Okay, I was impressed. This I could learn. It was exciting.

But the excitement wore off that evening as we rounded the point and sat in the Catalina Channel, drifting, no wind at all. I started to feel a little woozy. Soon I felt even worse, and for the first time in my life I was seasick

Maybe this wasn't the life for me, or at least that's what I was thinking as I went below to my berth. The boat was built for a crew of up to 10, so below decks the bunks lined the two sides of the companionway forward. My berth was the upper bunk second from the forward anchor locker. Patty's was the one below. She was in her bunk reading. "How's it going?" she asked, all innocent.

"I'm not feeling too hot," I replied. I am

going to lay down for awhile."

And the feeling kept getting worse. And worse. And worse.

Just about the time I was ready to upchuck my breakfast, Alan hollered from the deck down thru the companionway, "Hey, Bob, it's your turn on watch."

Watch? Was he kidding? All I was going to watch was how my digestive system could work in reverse. But, as they say, a mans gotta do what a mans gotta do. I never understood why that was, but it was.

And so I pried myself out of the bunk and wobbled up on deck. Alan looked at me and smiled. He smiled! What kind of a sadist had he turned into?

"Don't worry, it will go away. Just go over to the side of the boat and stick your finger down your throat. You'll feel better, I promise."

Yeah, right! That's what I want to do. Like hell! I'm not gonna let people see me being weak. Once more the "mans gotta do thing" entered my rapidly departing mind.

"Okay," he said. "Well, you're on for two hours." He pointed to the compass. "Just try to keep us on this course."

I looked, and the compass was pointed at 180°. I nodded, sat down and took the tiller. In the three months I'd sailed Rogue I understood you push it one way to go the other, so I didn't have much trouble staying on course. He watched for a few minutes (I guess he didn't trust me?) and then he turned to go down the companionway into the boat. As he turned he said once again, "You'd feel better if you go ahead and puke," and then he disappeared off the deck.

There was no wind and the boat was rocking. Soon it got to a point where I could not hold my gorge down any longer. I wrapped the little tiller line around the tiller and ran to the port side of the boat. I made it to within one or two steps from the rail when my reverse digestive system went into full gear. Fortunately, I was moving fast enough for it to make it over the side. For the next minute or so I watched as everything I had consumed for the past 40 years (or so it seemed) became fish food. I felt as if I could have won the projectile spewing contest in the Olympics!

But you know what? I did feel better. The headache wasn't as bad, the stomach wasn't upset, and all was good with the world. For about 20 minutes. Then I started to think I was gonna die.

Then I wished I would die.

Then I was afraid I wouldn't die!

Then I made another trip to the rail. This time it was just a lesson in futility. Try though I might, nothing came up but my expectations.

However, once again, I felt better. And once again, for about 20 minutes. By the end of my watch I was sure I had nothing left to throw up but my toenails.

This went on for two days. In those two days

we made less than 20 miles. We were still off the coast of Long Beach for God's sake! Catalina Island just sat there looking at us.

On my dog watch the second night, I looked longingly at the lights of Long Beach. I could make out the Queen Mary. I could see Parker's Lighthouse where I had downed numerous Terminal Island Iced Teas (that's an iced tea made with all the white liquors, a little coke, and then topped off with a float of Everclear) and spent many a fun night. And that's where I wanted to be. I was trying to think of how I could ask them to drop me off in Long Beach without looking like a wimp. I figured I would do it tomorrow. After all, we weren't going anywhere at this speed.

I headed down below after my watch for the few hours that remained until the next sunup. I opened my port (I was lucky, I had a port in my berth) and tried to go to sleep before I had to puke again.

And I did go to sleep. And then a miracle! When I awoke it was a whole new day, and a whole new life! I felt fine! I noticed that there was actually air coming thru the porthole. I wasn't seasick any more! In fact, I felt better than I had in a very long time.

As I walked into the galley area I saw the old coffee pot sitting on the gimbaled stove and poured myself a cup. It smelled great! I walked up onto the deck and Alan was on watch. He smiled.

"Feeling a little better today?" he asked.

"Yeah," I responded. "It's like I am a new me."

I sat down opposite him and we just sat there sipping coffee and enjoying a beautiful sunup.

After awhile I walked forward on deck. Life could not get any better, I thought. By now the breeze had come up and we were making about 5 knots on a due-south course. Our first planned stop would be Cabo San Lucas, and that was about 600 miles "down the road." I sat down on the edge of the inflatable dinghy looking out at the sea before us, and all of a sudden there were dolphin gliding along beside us riding the pressure of the bow wave.

I was home.

> Chapter 7 <
The Beginning of Understanding

We held a 180° course until the end of day 9. Alan pulled out the charts and was showing us where we were and then explained how he figured it out. This was my first lesson in navigation and it has stood me well over the last 35 years and 100,000 sea miles.

All you need to know is how fast you are going, how long you were going that fast and on what course. It seemed like a way too simplified way to navigate to me, but when we made our right angle towards Cabo, Alan said we were about 150 miles off. At the speed we were making that meant about another day and a half. It was now the afternoon.

I was starting to see why Alan had made such a big deal about keeping our log. After every watch, every two hours, whoever was coming off watch would have to enter the course held, the estimated speed (we had no knot meter, or any other electronics for that matter) and notes on the weather, sea state, and a short note. The notes got to be funny. Looking back at a ship's log can take you back to the day you made the entry. I find I still love reading old logs from trips and crossings I made.

On the morning of the third day we were passing Cabo Falso and sailing past a beautiful beach just around the famous rocks of the point at Cabo San Lucas. We sailed to the beach to anchor. We arrived just about the time Alan had said. Back in the day there was no marina in Cabo San Lucas. All cruising boats anchored on the beach. There was a river that came out there, but only the smaller pangas or dinghies could go up it. Cruisers usually landed right on the beach and then walked up to the village.

Anchoring on the beach was no simple matter. The beach dropped off very fast. It was steep and deep. The only way to anchor safely there was to

Stone Witch undersail

drop about 150 feet of chain with a good heavy anchor on the end (Stone Witch used a 150 lb. Danforth if I remember correctly) and then back up to the beach. Now that would be fairly easy for a boat with a motor, but here, once again, we got to watch a true master at work.

As we approached the beach we were under main and headsail only. When we were about 200 yards off Alan had us drop the main. We were doing about 2 knots. We had a couple of sweeps out just in case, but as it turned out, we never needed them. We then dropped the headsail. When we were about 100 feet off the beach he hollered to drop 150 feet of chain and he pushed the tiller hard a-port. The boat rounded up like a trained seal and when we came to rest, the stern was about 10 feet off the beach. "Toss the stern hook," he ordered, and a small (about 35 lb. Danforth) with 10 feet of chain and about 100 feet of 3/4" line was heaved over the stern. One of the crew jumped into the dinghy and took it ashore, dragging the anchor about 30 feet up the beach, and pushed it into the soft white sand.

I had done a little traveling prior to this. I'd ridden a Harley across Europe and all over the U.S., but I was not aware of the rules when you arrive by boat. Alan quickly explained that only the skipper should go ashore, and he would take all the passports, crew lists and ship's documents to the Harbor Master. Then he'd have to go see Aduana (Customs) and Imigra (Immigration).

Now you gotta remember, this was 40 years ago and in the '70s Cabo San Lucas was a very small and sleepy village. There were no paved roads and to make a phone call you had to walk up to the phone company. They would tell you a time to come back and then they would dial the number and guide you to a phone booth when the call was ready. Sometimes it would take a day or two.

As we sat on Stone Witch waiting for Alan to return, I saw a bunch of kids run over to the dinghy he'd left on shore. They jumped in it and started to push it into the water. I freaked! "Hey!" I shouted. "Get out of that boat, that's ours!"

Woody grabbed my arm. "Settle down," he said. "They are just going to play with it. They'll put it back when they are thru."

And sure enough, they laughed and played, jumping into the boat and diving off of it, and when they were thru they pushed it back up on the beach, cleaned it out, and went on their way down the beach again.

Being an Ugly American I had figured they were stealing it. He explained that here, where people don't have much, whatever is laying around is fair game to use or play with. And they would always return it.

A lesson learned.

Alan returned after a little over an hour and it was time for "shore leave." We checked the anchor to make sure we were good, and we all headed for shore.

> Chapter 8 <
My First Foreign Landfall

It seems kind of funny to me now, but I can remember the excitement as "the crew" went ashore and started into the village. Patty was wearing her normal attire from the boat, a bikini top and pair of skin-tight cutoff Levis shorts she had customized to make them look sexy. English Paul and Patrick wore cutoff Levi pants and T-shirts, and the tattoos on their arms stood out. Patrick had a Mexican senorita emblazoned on his arm, and English Paul had the list of girl's names down his arm, each one crossed out, with the last three the same name.

The regular crew were in shorts and tank tops, and I was wearing my black Levis, a black T-shirt with the sleeves cut off so you could see my tattoo "sleeves," and big silver rings on each finger with a heavy chain bracelet on my right wrist and a large leather watch band with spikes on it on my left. As you can tell from this, I was still dressing as if I were on a Harley instead of on a ship. That would change over time.

To get to the main road you went thru the Hacienda Hotel. At the time it was the only hotel on the beach and it welcomed anyone. After we passed thru the hotel we were on small roads that lead to the main road. We walked up to the main road, which was dirt, and up to the first palapa bar. We grabbed a table and soon were munching on tacos, downing cold cervezas and generally enjoying life!

As it turns out, I wish I had stayed a little longer. Cabo was never the same again. Over the next 20 years or so I would sail down about every two-three years. Each time Cabo was more and more civilized. Soon the streets were paved, there were a dozen expensive hotels, and even the Hacienda had been rebuilt and modernized. People had started settling there, and after the marina came in and Cabo Wabo (built by Sammy Hagar) was in the news, it became more like Southern San Diego. Now, the Cabo San Lucas Marina is the most expensive marina on the West Coast; more expensive than Newport, more expensive than Marina del Rey, and more expensive than the Portofino in Redondo Beach.

> Chapter 9 <
A Quick Trip to Reality,
and Back to Paradise Again

I still had my day job to consider with the magazine. I had to be in Daytona for motorcycle Speed Week.

You see, a few years earlier a good friend of mine, Bob Clark, had started a thing called "The Run to the Sun." In the late '60s he and Tom McMullen, the owner of AEE Choppers and Street Chopper Magazine, decided it would be kewl for a bunch of their readers to gather at the KOA in Valdosta, Georgia, and then ride in a pack to Daytona, where they had the roundy-round races (Flat Track.) Over the next couple years it grew to huge proportions. It might have had something to do with the depiction of the wet T-shirt contests that happened with regularity! I had been riding there from California for the past few years, and knew almost every one of the regulars.

So, as the boat sailed out of Cabo San Lucas, Patty and I boarded a plane and flew into Mexico

City and then on to Daytona Beach. Now, you want to talk about a change of pace? We flew from total peace and relaxation sailing down the west coast of the U.S. and Mexico into the turmoil of 35,000 bikers (it was much smaller then!) who were all doing their best to drain Daytona dry of all its alcoholic substances. And remember, this was the end of the '70s. Drugs were pretty much a way of life too.

The next week passed in a flash. I was hanging out with an old riding partner of mine, John "Rogue" Herlihey. He was the International President of the Huns, and they had obtained the use of a hotel. Aside from him being the

Bob & Patty aboard SV Stone Witch

club's IP he was also an ordained minister with the Universal Life Church. When he'd called to reserve the whole hotel he introduced himself as Reverend John Herlihey. Bet they were surprised.

Anyway, the festivities were pretty much 24/7 and another friend, Keith Ball, better known to Easyrider readers as Bandit, was also there. We rode the beaches, partied on Main Street, covered the bike shows and the Harley exhibits, and generally burned our candle at both ends.

It was a relief to get back on a plane and fly to Mazatlan to meet Stone Witch. They had stayed there after crossing the Sea of Cortez, waiting for us for a few days, and were anxious to head out. They had decided it was best to locate a little further up the coast where it was a little cleaner. You see, this was long before the El Cid Marina and Mazatlan Marina had been built. Since they didn't exist yet, Stone Witch had no choice but anchor in the main commercial harbor. This harbor had been formed by a large river that hits the sea at this point. The problem is, back then, the plumbing was not all it was cracked up to be in that part of Mexico. The boat was constantly surrounded by corn-backed lump-trout and finless browns, if you get my drift. It was a pleasure leaving the following morning and getting back to sea. We won't discuss what it was like pulling up the anchor chain and anchor. Suffice it to say everyone spent a little extra time washing their hands after it was done.

Our next stop was on Isla Isabel. This is a very small island about a mile in diameter, with a fresh water lake in the middle of it. Now don't go getting your hopes up. It is not a nice, clean, fresh water lake. Not in your wildest imagination. You see, frigates and boobies have been using this island for generations as a hatching ground for their young. In fact, while we were there, Jacques Cousteau had an encampment there doing a documentary on the island. It was uninhabited except for a few fishermen who set up a temporary village on the beach for the fishing season. The birds were absolutely not afraid of us and you could walk right up to them. The frigates had nests in the scrub trees and the boobies had their nests on the ground.

After Isla Isabel we sailed down to Punta Mita, and after spending a night sailed on to Puerto Vallarta. Puerto Vallarta was, even then, a bustling city. We anchored just inside the mouth of the harbor (much cleaner by the way!) and spent a week enjoying the sights and sounds of a pretty tourist town.

While we were there we heard about an Indian village by the name of Yelapa. It was not accessible by car, plane or bus. Only by water. We sailed the 8 miles and found a paradise that was about as perfect as a place could be: a perfect white beach with palapa restaurants and bars, and on the cliff was a small Indian village.

While kicking back with our feet in the sand

at one of the palapas and having a cold cerveza, we met a couple locals. They were from Redondo Beach! Where we were from! Talk about a small world. They invited us up to their house and it was a perfect escape: a palapa house covered with palm fronds, no windows and no locks on the doors. Best of all, there was no need for locks. This was a sleepy little village. Being an Indian village which was located in a reservation, the laws against smoking mota (marijuana) did not exist. Sitting at the beach, being served delicious tacos, well, it was a perfect life for the '70s.

But all good things must come to and end (I don't know quite why that is, but...) and so we hoisted the anchor once again and headed south. This time to Chemala Bay. Here we found two beautiful islands, Isla Colorado and Isla Passavera. These have probably the best snorkeling and diving on the Pacific Coast of Mexico. We

SV Stone Witch undersail off Mexico

dropped our hook right between the two islands, as they were only about 600 yards apart. The water was crystal clear and the white sand bottom was only 30 feet deep.

We kept moving further south. Soon we were in the tropics with 85° water matching the temperature of the air.

One of the fun pastimes aboard Stone Witch was to break out the 12-gauge shotgun for target practice. But first we had to set up the funnel-lator. This consisted of a length of surgical tubing run between the fore and aft shrouds, with a large funnel in the center. It would then be stretched across to the other side of the boat and a water balloon would be loaded into it. When released the water balloon would take off like a cannon shot. Each person took turns trying to hit balloons with the shotgun. It was also great in a water fight between boats!!

Hey, it broke the monotony and was a lot of fun!

Alan had a friend in the small town of Melaque, which is across a beautiful bay from Barra de Navidad. Philamina was an American who was married to a Mexican named Carlos, and she ran the place, which was a home away from home for cruisers. It was the first place cruisers would check in when arriving in the bay, and the last place they would check out. Boat names and images were painted all over the walls along with some very funny sayings. The funniest one

I recall (This was long before social correctness was a biggie): "Women do not belch, and women do not fart. Therefore they must bitch, or they will explode!"

Okay, so I'm a sickie, but I hit the floor laughing when I read that all those years ago.

I remember painting Stone Witch on the walls back then, and again years later when we sailed thru on the first Lost Soul, again on Predator, and again on Lost Soul II almost 30 years later. Philamina was still there, helping cruisers and making people feel at home.

Of course, back then Barra was just a sleepy village, as was Melaque. The Grand Bay Hotel had not been built, nor had the Grand Bay Marina been dredged out yet. But on the St. Patricio side (north), the anchorage was great, and Los Pelacanos was the place to go.

We took a side trip a few miles north for a day to see Tenecatita. This is still one of the most popular cruisers' hangouts in Mexico; a very well protected anchorage that could easily hold 100 boats. A small river of cool, clear water drains into the bay and you could take your dinghy up it for about two miles. It is overgrown with plant life and is one of the best dinghy adventures I can ever remember taking.

Now I have to tell you, before we took off on this voyage I had asked people what was best for trading fishermen for fish and lobster when cruising. Many experienced cruisers told me old

Playboys and Penthouse magazines traded well amongst the mostly male fishermen who were out for days at a time. As it turns out, I had a friend who worked at an adult book store. Once again, it was the '70s. Life was good! He gave me a box of old porn magazines which we shoved under one of the berths for trading goods. Fishermen would pull up, and not a word would be spoken. They would hold up their catch, we would hold up a couple copies of Big Juggs & Ugly Mugs and viola! We had more fish than we knew what to do with!!

Oh, yeah, and it was sailing from the Tenecatita anchorage back to Melaque about 25 years later that Stone Witch sank. (No, I was not aboard!) She hit a rock rounding the point and went down in less than 30 minutes. She still sits there today, as a diver's haven.

But then again, I have digressed. Sorry 'bout that.

The crew (l to r) Dan, Woody, Alan & Patrick

> Chapter 10 <
A Movie Set and Historical Tacos

A few miles down the beach was the large Bay of Manzanillo. This is a place you can get just about anything you need for your boat, as it is a large commercial fishing center. But north of the commercial area is a little place called Las Hades. Las Hades is paradise! In fact, for those of you who are old enough to remember the movie "10" with Bo Derek, it was actually being filmed there about the time we were anchored off the beach.

I remember putting a credit card on file at the front desk and for the next few days we lived the life of movie stars, laying by the pool and having a drink brought to us by men in turbans (really!), or kicking back on a covered lounge on the beach, looking out at the boat anchored just a few hundred feet off the beautiful white beach. I was starting to think I could really get into this sailing thing.

But once again we were off. This time for one of the places Alan had been talking about since we

left Redondo Beach - Zihuatanejo. This was a real
eye opener. As some of you may know, in 1542
Captain Juan Rodriguez Cabrillo sailed into San
Diego, thus "discovering" San Diego. (I guess the
Indians that lived there hadn't seen it??) Anyway,
as it turns out, the boats that Cabrillo sailed were
built in Zihuatanejo. As we walked thru the old
marketplace we were walking the same worn out
paths that ol' Juan was walking. When we stopped
for a taco and sat at the stone tables that had been
there for hundreds of years, we might have been
spilling taco sauce on the same spot that ol' Juan
spilled his taco sauce! How kewl is that?

I was starting to evolve into a sailor. By the
time we were in Zihuat I had learned the names
of the lines on the boat. I knew a halyard from
a sheet, and a topping lift from a downhaul. But
better yet, I knew just about every job on the boat
and was really getting into navigation. Alan even
tried to teach me celestial, but that was way over
my head at the time. I did manage to pick it up
later, but that's another story. Of course, I was a
deck hand and not a rigging guy. At 275 pounds I
was not one they asked to climb the ratlins. Nay,
nay I say, not I. That is work for the little guys.
Not that we had many little guys on the crew. I
still (and to this day) have never seen the top of a
mast while standing upon it. And I have absolutely
no desire to do so.

So, one sunny day we are kicking back on
the boat while anchored in Zihuat and Alan says,

"Let's invite the cruisers over for a party."

He didn't have to say it twice. The crew split up, with Patrick going ashore to try and find a musician while the rest of us headed out to the 8-9 cruising boats that were anchored there.

Now, once again, it is time for a small world story. I pull alongside a Nor'Sea 27, which is a small pocket cruiser that is still very popular today, and knock on the hull. A man sticks his head out and says hi.

I looked at him, he looked at me, and I said, "Don't I know you?"

"Bob," he said, "you still dressing like a biker? What are you doing down here?"

His name was (and is) Dean Wixom, and I had known him a couple years earlier. I'd met him while I was working as an editor at Cycle News. The Wixom Brothers were one of our advertisers and they made fairings, the things that police bikes have as a dashboard, where the windshield mounts.

Anyway, it seems that unbeknown to me, he was also building a new class of cruising sailboat, the Nor'Sea 27. When he completed the first hull he claimed it. Then he sold about 10 more and sold them to make enough money to go cruising. And so it was that two old bikers sat there on his first Nor'Sea 27 and got ready for a party aboard the most beautiful ship in the harbor, Stone Witch.

The party could not have been a bigger success. The band from the waterfront hotel came out to supply the music and everyone from every cruising boat, as well as guests from the beach hotels and even locals and businessmen, all came. We must have had 60-70 people on board. Everyone brought something for the "potluck" and one of the locals brought a shit-load of tequila and limes. Kerosene lights lined the deck and as dark descended, so did an alcohol fog.

The party went on until the wee hours of the morning. When it was over we seemed to have lost English Paul and gained a local businessman. The next day we found Paul, as he had hooked up with a girl who was staying at the hotel and he had opted for a room with running water and electricity. The businessman, it seems, had gone swimming at some time during the party and his clothes were hanging to dry. He was wrapped in a blanket. As it turned out, he had also lost his Rolex watch.

Now, as I said before, I had asked some sailors what was the best thing to take to trade for lobster and fish. Aside from the porno books they said perfume for the ladies, fishing gear for the men, and cheap watches. Down below I had a $25 knock-off of a Rolex. I took the man below decks, opened my "trade bag" and pulled out one of the fake Rolexes. I swear he started to get tears in his eyes.

"No." I said rapidly, "it's not real. It's a knock off... a fake."

He said he understood, but still, for me to

Party on board Stone Witch in Zihuatanejo

give him this watch meant a lot to him. He tried to give me money, but I wouldn't take it. And that meant a lot to me. I was starting to learn what it takes to be a real cruiser. Being able to help someone is much more fulfilling than besting someone in a business deal. This was my first lesson. But it would not be my last.

> Chapter 11 <
Onward to Acapulco, a Little
Decadence and a "perfect" Village

It was hard to leave Zihuatanejo. We had made a lot of friends there and as I was learning, the joy of departing on a new leg of your adventure was often outweighed by the leaving of good friends.

Of course, the other side of that coin is, the more you cruise, the more you realize that where cruisers hang out is limited by facilities, so as long as two boats are heading in the same direction they will keep bumping into each other.

We decided it was time we headed down to Acapulco. Plans were made to depart a little after dawn the next day. We'd noticed that there was a little offshore breeze that would come up as the land warmed from the sun coming up from the east, and we wanted to take advantage of that offshore to start us on our 118-mile trip to Acapulco.

We found Paul and let him know we would be

leaving at 9:00 a.m. sharp, as he was staying with his new lady friend at her fancy hotel. He said not to worry. He would be ready at 9 sharp.

After breakfast the next morning we started getting prepared to haul anchor. When you are on Stone Witch hauling the anchor meant just that; manually lifting the 120 feet of 3/8" chain and the 150 pound anchor at the end of it.

If Alan was anything, he was prompt. Paul had not shown up yet and Alan pretty much said if he missed the boat he'd have to find a way down to Acapulco, our next port. Just about the time the anchor was pulled and tied on deck to lock it down for the voyage we saw Paul running down the beach. Trailing a few yards behind him and running just as hard was his lady-friend, and she was hauling two suitcases. Patrick looked up and smiled.

"Oh oh, it looks like Paul is up to his old tricks."

It seems that back in Redondo, Paul had a bit of a reputation with the ladies. Thus the chain of names running down his arm. He was a true believer in "love 'em and leave 'em."

Patrick jumped into the dinghy and headed to meet Paul. You could hear Paul yelling at Patrick, "Dude, hurry up! She thinks she's going with us!"

Yup, Paul had been telling her for days, as she paid for his drinks, his meals and just about everything else, that she would be cruising with them down the coast. You see, Paul didn't have any money. He had not even chipped in for the voyage, but he was a good friend of Patrick's so we'd let him come.

Paul may not have had any money, but he looked like a rock star of that era: long blonde hair, a blonde mustache, well built, and often mistaken for Eddie Van Halen. A mistake, by the way, which he was known to foster at times if it would get him an advantage, or get him laid.

Well, they did get off the beach before she could catch him and I have to say, I felt pretty bad for her standing there on the beach, bags in hand, as Stone Witch sailed off the hook and the topsail was opened and braced.

The sail from Zihuatanejo to Acapulco was one of those dream sails. It was about 125 miles and Alan figured we'd get in just before dawn, but he knew the harbor entrance pretty well and it was well lit. The sea gods, however, had different ideas. It seems there was a 3-5 knot current running down the coast, and with the 10-15 knot wind on our tail, with all the sails flying, we were making about 7-8 knots over the water, and closer to 10 -12 knots over the ground. So it was to be a quick trip.

By 10:00 p.m. we were only about 10 miles out of Acapulco. Patty and I were up on the bowsprit watching a pod of dolphins that were riding our bow wake, and the water was full of fluorescent plankton.

"Wow! It's like being on acid," I said to Patty

as we watched in awe. The sun had set but the sky was still a dark pink blending to a dark blue. The winds were about 8-10 knots, but we were moving at about 7, so it was as if we were on a calm sea.

"Yeah," Patty replied. "Too bad we don't have any. This would be cool."

And then it hit me. When we had been in Daytona it happened that my birthday fell on the Saturday night we were hitting Main Street. I remembered one of the people we were partying with gave me a small little plastic bag. It had 4 hits of Blue-Dot acid. We'd taken two to celebrate that night, but then I didn't remember ever taking the other two.

"Wait here a minute," I told Patty, "I'll be right back."

I went down to my berth and found my cutoffs. Sure enough, tucked into a little stash pocket I'd sewn into the hem there was the little baggy, and inside were two little tabs of Blue-Dot.

A few minutes later Patty and I were laying on our bellies on the deck, with our heads hanging over the side, watching the light show being created by the dolphin as they rode our bow wave in the phosphorescent waters. It seemed like forever, but it couldn't have been more than an hour. As we looked up we saw the lights of Acapulco off in the distance. It was a magic night.

I hardly even remember as we pulled into the entrance of Acapulco and sailed around to the North Bay to anchor. It was much bigger and had a lot more lights than I expected.

In the morning we went ashore to do some restocking and then we pulled alongside the dock at the Acapulco Yacht Club to fill our water tanks. The town was too large and too expensive to hang out in, so we cut our stay there short and soon were on our way further south. Our next stop was Puerto Escondido. This was a truly unforgettable experience.

Puerto Escondido was, at that time, one of the best "off the beaten track" surf spots in the world. It was also where Patrick met Maria, the lady that would become a part of our cruising family for the next month.

The village of Puerto Escondido was a perfect little village. The dirt streets were clean, the tiendas (stores) were well stocked, and the prices were not tourist prices. But the cafés... the cafés were the real treat. Each one we tried was better than the last. I remember sitting with Patty in a little café right on the beach eating turtle steaks (okay, it was the '70s and that was kewl!).

What was odd was the fact that there were a couple fishermen who had just landed on the beach next to us, and we watched as they pulled out a couple of huge turtles. They flipped them on their backs and walked into town. I asked the man who was the owner of the café we were in what they were doing. He informed us that the most humane way to kill turtles, so they could be butchered, was to lay them on their back until they stopped breathing.

So, we sat there eating steaks made from probable relatives of the poor guys laying out there in the sun. Patty felt sorry for them, so she took a small piece of the turtle steak she was eating and fed it to one of the turtles on the beach. Seemed a little odd to me.

While we were there we ran into a large contingent of American and Australian surfers. There is a very long beach across from the anchorage that was known for some of the best surfing in the world. The Pacific swells were unimpeded as they swept across from as far away as Japan and China. Lining El Morrow Beach (that means "the nose" in Spanish) were dozens of surf shacks. Before long we were invited to join them surfing. Being from Southern California, it was pretty much a necessity. Soon we lost track of time, spending a night or two at the surf shacks and then on the boat. It was a magical few days we spent in Puerto Escondido.

But we were starting to get close to some real adventure. Alan had told us that one of the major crossings we'd be making would be the crossing of the Gulf of Tehuantepec. This was the land of the Tehuantepecer, a wind that seems to come up from out of nowhere and blows out of the north at up to 100 mph. But we still had a couple stops before we'd wait to do the crossing.

We had one adventure while we were under sail on our way to Puerto Angel. One evening we were all sleeping in our bunks like good boys and girls when we were awakened by an odd movement of the boat. It felt as if we were sailing backwards. It was especially disturbing for Alan. You see, his bunk was in the aft cabin, and since we were in the tropics he usually kept the aft window open a bit for fresh air, unless we were in rough weather when he would close it. Well, we were in perfect weather so he slept soundly with the window open... until he got hit in the face with sea water!

He jumped out of the bunk after closing the hatch and made his way topside. There he found English Paul passed out. And he was supposed to be on watch. Now, he was not just sleeping on the job. That would have been too easy. No, it seems that earlier, while everyone was asleep, he had happened upon the medical kit. Now, the Stone Witch is an ocean going vessel and it had an ocean

Patrick checking the sails while Alan is at the helm

going vessel's medical kit. You know, the real emergency stuff, like splints, sutures, large rolls of gauze, and, oh yeah, a lot of drugs. One of which was morphine. Morphine is used when someone is really in a bad way, and it is a necessity on an ocean going vessel.

Now, if there was one thing old Paul was into it was opiates of any kind, morphine being one of his favorites. And so he had opened a fresh packet containing a syringe, filled it with the medicinal morphine and proceeded to empty it into his veins. And then, like a good lad, he headed up on deck to his post, where he promptly went "on the nod" as they say, and passed out. This allowed Stone Witch to choose her own course of action and she decided it was time to see if she could sail backwards, with the topsail flying! Of course, once she had started her backwards journey, the bow wave became a stern wave, thus pushing a few hundred gallons of nice, cool sea water thru the aft port and right onto Alan's bunk.

Now I have to admit, Alan had a lot more composure in the situation than I might have had. He didn't blow it! He quietly sent Paul below to consider his ill-advised actions, and took over the tiller duties for the rest of Paul's Shift. I seriously believe if it had been up to me, at that point in my life, I would have steered toward shore, and once I was a mile or so offshore I would have given Paul his walking papers, or in that case, his swimming papers. But Alan was, and always has been, part saint and he let it pass.

And then there was Woody Le Mar's birthday. Now Woody was not a normal person. He was pretty much more sea creature than seaman. His whole life revolved around the sea and he was the man who I first heard the description of "Cruisian." I'd asked him what nationality he was, and that was his answer. Cruisian. I liked it and still use that term today!

So one morning, as we were still heading down the coast, it was Woody's birthday. Patty had whipped up some kind of a muffin and had a candle in it for him. After breakfast he went up on deck, and in a few minutes we heard a bunch of whopping and hollering coming from topside. There were a bunch of dolphin swimming on the bow. Nothing really strange or odd about that, but what was strange and odd was Woody had climbed down onto the dolphin-striker. That was a chain that ran from a connection on the waterline out to the end of the huge bowsprit. Well, somehow Woody had climbed down there and was whooping and hollering as the dolphins would jump out of the water, and he could actually reach out and touch them. This went on for about 10 minutes and then the dolphin headed out to wherever they had been going.

But Woody was ecstatic! You couldn't get the grin off his face with a sledge hammer.

"Can you believe it" he stammered. "They must have known it was my birthday and came by to see me."

And I think he probably still believes that to this day! And so do those of us who were on board that magic day.

> Chapter 12 <
A Surprise Fiesta, and I Learn What Kedging Is

The Tehuantepecer is caused by a very narrow strip of land, the narrowest of all Mexico. It is just 135 miles across. North of the narrow strip of land is the Gulf of Mexico. South is the Gulf of Tehuantepec and the Pacific Ocean. So if you happen to be out in the gulf it is very possible that this 100 mph wind can come up in less than an hour. So the local wisdom is to stay with "one foot on the beach," which means stay at about the 100 foot deep line just off the beach. That way if it does come up the seas won't be able to build. You can pull up to the beach, drop a hook and sit and get sandblasted for awhile, but it usually doesn't last more than a day or two.

So Alan decided we would go to Puerto Madero, which is just about the last place in Mexico to clear out. That was about a 250-mile run across the Gulf of Tehuantepec.

At dawn (why is it sailors always have to leave at dawn!?) Stone Witch hoisted anchor and we headed out. The weather reports expected fair weather for the next three days so we sailed as tight as we could to Puerto Madero. As it turned out the crossing was anything but calm. We never did see the Tehuantepecer but it ended up taking 10 days to sail the 250-mile passage.

Here is the way Dan recalls it, some 35 years later: "I recall several intense lightning storms with bolts dancing all around the Stone Witch. I remember having fin whales come over and check us out for about an hour. I had an eyeball to eyeball encounter with one as he (or she) emerged from under the hull, his eyeball being the size of a basketball. Standing watch at night, the sky was as clear as a sky could get, and looking up and seeing the moon come out from behind the main topsail could give you goosebumps."

On our arrival in Puerto Madero, there was an estuary about a mile long and about 800 feet wide that we would have to sail into. Patrick's lady-friend, Maria, also our official translator, translated the directions we were getting from the hand-cranked radio. Once we sailed a mile into the channel we were to make a slight turn to starboard and into a lagoon where we could anchor and do all of our clearance out of Mexico. I had to admire the way Alan just took it all in. He had us drop the dinghy and he took it into the channel and then back out.

"Looks okay to me," he said, and with that he took the tiller in hand and started giving orders for which sails to raise, which to lower, and we were all way to busy to be worried about it.

The boat drifted down the channel at about 4-5 knots without a problem. Just about a mile in, a channel showed off to the starboard at about 30°. Alan deftly maneuvered Stone Witch into mid channel and gave the order to drop all sail. The sails came down and the anchor was at the ready. Just about the middle of the lagoon we dropped the hook and sat back to admire where we were.

Talk about a sheltered anchorage. It was completely cut off from the sea. The water was like glass, yet a slow breeze kept the area fairly cool.

Maria went in with Alan in case any translation was needed to handle the clearance into the new port. We hauled buckets of saltwater on deck and washed her down. After awhile Alan and Maria came back aboard with some good news. There was going to be a festival in the town of Puerto Madero tonight. The biggest of the year!

We all washed up with saltwater, and the ladies even rinsed their hair with a little fresh water, which was a first for awhile as fresh water was precious on the boat. We put on our best and headed into town.

It seemed really strange to be walking down this dirt road, a thousand miles from home, but feel as if we were home. We said "Ola" to people that we passed in the road, and soon a couple who came out of a house and were heading to the fiesta had joined us. Maria explained that we had sailed in on "el Grande Barco" and they were full of questions. We'd been in Mexico for a couple months by now and I was starting to understand a lot of what was being said.

And then we came upon the festival. It was great! They had booths setup with darts and balloons, and lots of different foods, some of which I had never seen before. Everyone was happy and smiling, and it was like being at a fair at home, only better.

The night air was perfect. Patty looked great and couldn't stop smiling. Patrick and Maria walked off in one direction, Paul and the crew headed over to the cerveza truck, while Alan, Patty and I wandered around just enjoying the festivities.

Later that evening we walked slowly back to the boat. I can still remember how the music from the fiesta was wafting across the village and we could still hear it on the boat. It gave a surreal feeling to being there. The stars were above us, the weather was perfect, and once again, we experienced one of life's perfect moments.

When morning came there was only one missing member and no one was surprised. Paul had met a "lady of the evening" last night and ended up going to her place. As we progressed further south this would become a standard practice for him. He'd meet a hooker, promise to take her to America, and then stay with her until the boat was ready to leave, when he'd "go out for a pack of cigarettes" and never return.

We stayed a few days and got to know some of the locals. It was an idyllic time and we really started to feel like locals as opposed to tourists. I was picking up more and more Spanish and the "real world" back home seemed like it was a thousand miles away.

And, as a matter of fact, it was!

Wait! We were heading to Guatemala. We weren't there yet, but we were starting to get close!

First we had to get out of the estuary and there was something odd we had discovered while we stayed in Puerto Madero. There was never an offshore breeze! There was either no breeze or an onshore breeze. But no offshore! And it was here I learned the all-important sailing method called kedging.

Checking out of Mexico at Puerto Madero

Okay, first I have to tell you, kedging is NOT fun! Oh, I know, I often spout off about how the difference between an ordeal and an adventure is attitude, but keeping a good attitude thru this was beyond mere mortal men. You see, here's how it works. A bunch of you get on the foredeck with a second anchor, a bunch of chain and a bunch of line. Then you lower the 75-lb. hunk of iron down to two men in the dinghy. They then pile the chain in the dink and take it as far up the estuary as possible. Usually about 150 feet.

Now here is where the fun comes in. They drop the anchor over the side and feed the chain out as fast as they can. You see, it's an inflatable dinghy, and you can't let the chain just "play out," as it would cut right thru the dinghy.

Okay, so now the crew who were left on board start hauling in the line that is attached to the chain, which is, in turn, attached to the anchor. But first you have to pull in enough line to "set" the anchor. So you haul, and you haul, and you haul. Finally, when you have about 100 feet of the line on board, you feel it set. So now you get to pull the 74-foot boat and all aboard, using your aching arms and back, forward.

But wait! Haven't you forgotten something? Oh yes, the anchor. You still have an anchor down. So a couple of the crew haul the anchor in, while the rest of the crew pull the boat forward. About 30-40 feet. Then you feel the new anchor start to drag as there is very little scope out. Once again, now you lower the larger anchor into the dinghy. And once again the chain, and the line. Once again the "drop crew" takes the anchor out as far as they can and drop it overboard.

After we had done this most of the morning we had managed to move the boat about 100 feet. At that rate we'd be doing it for a week.

Okay, before you say it, why didn't we try pushing the boat out with the dinghy and outboard? We did and it wouldn't move it. It had about a 5hp outboard and it just didn't have enough power.

Finally, after a few more futile tries, Alan jumped into the dinghy and headed over to the fishing shacks that lined the shore. In a few minutes he was being followed back to the boat by a fishing panga with a 125hp outboard on the back. We tossed him a line and he wrapped it around a post near the back of the panga and slowly turned on the throttle. As soon as we started moving Alan had us haul the anchor, and soon we were moving at a stead 2-3 knots out of the estuary and into the open waters of the Pacific.

We waved goodbye to our friend in the panga, who had probably made enough that afternoon to take all of the villagers to a taco feast, and we set sail for new waters and new adventures.

> Chapter 13 <
Land of the Guatermellon

As we set sail we entered Guatemalan waters. To me this was now a true adventure. In the '70s Central America was forbidden fruit. All the news coming out of that area was bad news. Little did we know most of it was being caused by the CIA, NSA and a bunch of other USA initials. All we'd seen or heard on TV and the radio was Southern Guatemala and El Salvador were places to be avoided. Not being the brightest bulbs in the pack, that was right where we were heading. How else would we be able to experience adventure, right?

One thing you might notice if you look at a chart of Guatemala is that there are really no sheltered anchorages. It's mostly open beach, and mostly open to the pacific swells.

We made one stop, and don't hold me to this, but I think it was the small town of Tahuexco. We stopped there for a couple days, got some water and beer, and headed back out again. But I do remember, "thru a bit of a fog after all these years" meeting some people who had a condo a mile or so up the beach, and they invited us to come to a party there. Now here, I have to admit, there was some very good herb being offered, and I think we had a real good time that night, but I couldn't swear to it.

By the way, speaking of swearing... I just need to let you know up front, sailing, when it became my way of life, probably saved my life. Because it is what helped me stop smoking pot and a bunch of other things we don't need to go into here. But this I can say without fear of leading you astray... Once sailing becomes a lifestyle, the high you get sailing will far exceed anything you get artificially.

Okay, enough preaching, back to reality!

The next day, with my head still swimming in some artificial reality, we hoisted anchor and headed for the Port of San Jose. Rumor had it the anchoring there was good, and from there we could take a bus and explore Guatemala. As it turned out, the rumors were not quite factual. The anchorage was not just poor, but it was the worst any of us, even Alan, had ever had to endure. Today there is a dredged harbor and breakwater to make things more tenable, but back in the '70s it was open beach with a dirty river flowing into it and a long pier. The pier is where they loaded cotton on to huge ships that were anchored there and private boats were not allowed near it, nor were our dinghies.

Once again, this was the late '70s, and the Cold War was in full swing. When we dropped anchor we were just a few hundred yards off a huge Russian freighter awaiting her load of cotton. The problem with the anchorage was the wind and swells. They did not want to agree. There was a strong wind running onshore for half the day, and offshore half the day. This kept the boat pointed north or south (at that point the coast runs east and west) and the Pacific swells, which were huge, were running out of the west, unimpeded all the way from the orient.

This was a first for me, and I have to tell you, not something any of us liked in the least. You see, what would happen is the swells would build up a rhythm and every few minutes the boat would start rocking back and forth until (and I swear this is true!), the tips of the yards were within a few feet of touching the sea, first on the port side, then on the starboard, port, starboard, port, starboard. This would put the cabin sole onto at least a 50°-60° tilt. You could not stand. You had to brace yourself, and walking was almost impossible.

Somehow we got the dinghy launched and hoped things would calm down after we spent a few hours in town. The town of San Jose, at that time, was one street. It lead straight off the pier and went for about a half-mile with what looked like board sidewalks from the old west, and rag-tag buildings, all of which looked like they were falling down. They were crammed tight against each other, and I swear half of them were bars and half were whore houses. At least that's what it seemed like in my feeble recollection of that first day.

The people on the streets all looked like sailors off the ships, or those who loaded the ships. They were shorter in stature than people we had met sailing south, and they all wore big belt buckles and large hats, probably to keep the sun off them. Not to be indelicate, but we ended up calling them "Four Foot Machos" because they all tried to look so macho.

Oh, yeah, and the streets were full of armed soldiers everywhere. And the headlines on the local newspapers were not hindered by censorship. The lead story the day we landed was about a machete attack in some village, with some extremely graphic and grizzly photos on the cover. Pictures of people with their arms, legs and heads chopped off!

It did give one a feeling that we were not in Kansas any more!

Now Patty, not being a world traveler (like I was???) had opted to wear her tightest Danskin top and tightest Levis, and her cowboy hat. The Machos who were on the street just stopped and stared at her as we walked by. I think it was a good thing there were 5-6 of us and that we were all pretty big, or there might have been some trouble. Most of them were carrying machetes.

The first bar we saw that looked like it served

food, we went in. It was dark, but it had a few tables and soon we were enjoying some cold cervezas and munchies. Before we'd left the place Paul had met a hooker, convinced her he was going to "take her away from all this" and had a place to stay. The rest of us wandered up and down the street for awhile, and then headed back to the boat to see if it had calmed down.

It had not! In fact, it had gotten worse if that was possible. With the dinghy pulled along side, if you waited for the side you were boarding to roll your way, you could just step out of the dinghy onto the cap rail. The next few seconds it would be like an elevator, shooting you up almost 10 feet before it would start to roll back again.

Below decks was an absolute disaster. Dishes, pots and pans had worked themselves out of the cabinets, and people's sea bags had fallen from their berths. There was debris everywhere you looked.

So we decided that maybe a few days off the boat might do us some good. We found that there was a bus stop about a mile up the dirt road where it met the highway, so we hustled back aboard the boat and got some traveling gear and then we hoofed it to the highway. There we boarded the first bus that came thru. We didn't recognize any of the towns it was headed for, but that didn't matter. We were going to explore and have an adventure.

And that is how we ended up crossing into El

Salvador!

As we bounced along the road we were so busy looking at the passing scenery, I guess we didn't see the signs until we saw the one saying "Alto-Aduana El Salvador." Now, I wasn't that fluent yet with the language, but there was no missing that we were about to enter El Salvador, which at that time had bands of teenagers roaming the streets with machine guns.

Oops!

We did manage to get off and go back across the border into Guatemala, and then caught the first bus to a city we could understand - Guatemala City! Along the road on the trip to the city we were passed by a dozen jeeps and trucks, all filled with teenagers and some that might have been younger than that, in uniform and carrying rifles. We couldn't wait to get to the city where we thought we might feel a little safer.

Guatemala City was just that. A city. We walked the streets for an hour or so and ran into some hippies. They told us that we should go to Antigua, the old Capital City. They said not to miss the ferry ride to a small island where there was a small café that specialized in hash-filled brownies.

Okay, once again, I gotta cop to the fact that this was the '70s, remember?

The bus ride to Antigua will never be forgotten by any of us. The fact that we made it alive was a complete surprise. The bus we got on had seen better days and was probably pre-WWII. It was packed with people, chickens, pigs, and luggage tied on to the roof like Ma and Pa Kettle. Once on the bus the driver started driving over roads that were at times nothing more than cattle trails. One of the people on the bus told Patrick, thru Maria, that there were so many earthquakes in the Antigua region that they stopped maintaining the roads years ago when they moved the capital to Guatemala City. At one point there was a switchback, but the lower part of the switchback had dropped about 15 feet over the years. The bus driver simply dropped down a gear, floored it, and when he hit the end of the paved road he swung it hard to the right, up the hillside, and the inertia kept the bus on the dirt cliff long enough for it to flip around, heading in the new direction on the road 15 feet higher than the road below!

But we did arrive alive! We walked the quaint streets for a bit and found an old hotel where the rooms didn't look too bad. I also remember it was extremely inexpensive. In fact, the place was very popular with Europeans. There were probably as many Europeans as there were Guatemalans. The reason was simple. Most meals in the small shops would run you about a dollar. Seriously! Huevos Rancheros were a buck. A couple tacos and a beer? A buck! It was great.

Oh yeah, and there were no laws about pot back then in the town. People walked the streets and would stop to talk, pass a joint, and then walk on. And every Wednesday, like clockwork, a small boat would pull up to the dock and people would pack on, paying a dollar each way to go to Maria's on a small island just off the coast. When they arrived there they would have a couple tacos followed up by a hash-filled brownie or two, and then take a leisurely boat ride back to Antigua for the evening.

It was an idyllic town until one night when one of the hundreds of earthquakes that hit the town every year took place. Even being from California where earthquakes were a way of life, the ones in Antigua were of a whole new magnitude. We couldn't wait to leave the next morning.

For the trip back to San Francisco the plan was for Stone Witch to go offshore a few hundred miles, in fact, about halfway to Hawaii in order to avoid the headwinds. Patrick, Maria, Patty and I decided to make other arrangements as we didn't have the time to make a 35-40 day trip. Patty opted to take a train all the way thru Mexico with Maria, who was going to stop by her home in Mexico City, show her around, and then go on up to the states by train. That sounded like an adventure to Patty. Patrick and I opted to fly out of Guatemala City, and flew home in a few hours.

But the saga of Stone Witch doesn't end here. You see, since Paul didn't have the funds for a plane ticket, he had to sail back with Stone Witch. I don't know who disliked this arrangement more,

him or the captain and crew. But he did sign on.
They made a brief stop on their way northwest in
Puerto Escondido. As it turns out, the young lady
Paul had left standing on the beach in Zihuatanejo
was now staying in a quaint little bungalow in that
town. Paul hooked up with her. She forgave him
and then bought him a ticket to Los Angeles so
they could fly there together. How nice!

Except when they arrived at LAX, Paul
called Melissa, his old girlfriend of three times,
and asked her to pick them up at the airport. As
it turned out, Melissa's car was not running, so
her mother gave her a ride to pick Paul up, not
knowing, of course, that he'd brought home a
friend. Rumor has it not a word was said on the
10-minute ride from LAX back to their home in
Redondo Beach.

They pulled into the driveway, Melissa, her
mother, Paul, and Paul's new-found friend. As
they got out of the car Paul said, "I'm out of
cigarettes. I'm going down to the corner for some.
Anybody want anything?"

And that was the last time English Paul was
seen in Redondo Beach.

> Chapter 14 <
In Search of the Perfect Liveaboard.

As soon as I was back in Redondo I started looking for a boat. A good cruising boat. I didn't have much money, but after a week or two I found a Newport 30-II that was in good condition and was not too expensive. About $15,000. I made arrangements with the owner of El Sueno to carry the paper on it and soon I had my cruising boat. She was in a slip in King Harbor which was only a block away from my house behind the head shop (and ½ block off Hermosa Beach!). I had a two-car garage another block away where I kept my old 74 El Dorado and my motorcycles. I still had a few bikes, like my Harley, an all-black Fatbob with ape hangers and up-swept fishtails which I named "The Black Bitch", and my 1945 Indian restored army bike. I also had a couple of project bikes I was working on with the motorcycle magazines I worked for.

While we were cruising on Stone Witch, everyone that was out there was on smaller boats.

I never figured I could have a boat like Stone Witch, but I could get a good cruising boat.

It was here I learned a very important lesson. Other people's idea of a perfect boat is not necessarily what you want. When you are 6'4" and weigh in at over 250 pounds (hey, I was younger then and hadn't gained my "adult" weight yet!) you need a larger boat than the average bear. I was in my mid thirties and pretty active. Living at the beach makes for an active lifestyle: riding my bike (bicycle) on the strand to check out the hotties, working out at Gold's Gym (there was only one back then, in Santa Monica) and pretty much burning the candle at both ends. But since the wisdom of the day was to cruise in a small boat, I got a small boat.

Of course, I had to make a few changes first. El Sueno (The Dream) was a decent enough name for most people's boats, but at the time I did not feel like other people. So the first thing I did was to paint over the old name with her new name - Outlaw. That fit me!

I have to admit I did like sailing her. It was so easy after sailing the Witch. She had a one-lung diesel that you hand-started with a pull rope, and raising the sails was a one-man job. Every chance I got I would take her out of the slip and go day-sailing. I felt like a seasoned cruiser after the voyage to Guatemala. The people on the dock even started to talk to me as if I were a real person.

Of course, I was blackballed from the local club, King Harbor Yacht club. Oh, it was all innocent enough, but a guy I'd met down the dock named Roger Wine had the largest boat on that dock. I think it was a 38-40' Hatteras. Anyway, after awhile we became buddies. One day he came to me and asked if he could borrow my motorcycle boots and chain belt-buckle. The yacht club was having a costume party, and he wanted to go as a biker. Well, I was well equipped for such a task. He was about my size, so I loaned him my Biker News cutoff with all the paraphernalia that it included: the belt, boots and a T-shirt we sold out of the magazine that said, "Bikers have more fun than people."

Outlaw undersail off King Harbor. The original name was El Sueno, and it didn't fit the new owner!

85

The evening of the party I happened to be walking up the dock to my bike when we ran into each other. He was on the way to the club. I thought a great way for him to arrive, as a biker, was to be riding on the back of a Harley. So I offered him a ride. He jumped at the idea.

As we rode around the harbor to the yacht club he was laughing his ass off. He was having a ball. So I figured I'd give him a little extra boost towards winning the costume prize. When we came to the bottom of the outside little stairway (there were 4-5 steps up to a landing), I wicked on the throttle and popped a small wheelie, bringing the front wheel enough off the ground so as to clear the first couple steps. Then as the rear wheel hit them I wicked on the throttle just enough to get

Bob & Degenerate jim messing about on boats!

86

us onto the landing, where I made a hard left and stopped right in front of the main doorway.

Roger was having a ball, and people were laughing and pointing as I turned back down the stairs after he got off, and headed down and out the driveway. But there were those who did not approve of such shenanigans, and a year later, when Roger put me up for membership, I was black-balled.

Funnier yet, many years later, after a couple of my books had come out about sailing and after we had a successful sailing magazine, they sent a delegation over to my office across the channel to ask me to be a member. By then I had been a member of the Hawaii Yacht Club for years, so I politely declined.

But I did notice I actually started to change some. At the time I was reading books like Landfalls in Paradise by Earl Hinz, and Cruising Seraffyn by Lin & Larry Pardey. Little did I know that years later they would all become good friends... But I digress.

So here I was with this 30-foot monohull and I was sailing all the time. But it wasn't the same as it was on Stone Witch. I would keep remembering the smell of the boat; the mixture of kerosene, diesel (from the stove), Stockholm tar that coated the rigging, and a little mold. It was the smell of the sea and I missed it. Oh, I tried to make Outlaw salty. But it was all to no avail. I bought oil lamps down at Minney's Chandlery and even put

baggywrinkles in the rigging. But no mater what
I did it looked like a little yellow sailboat. It was
cute. Cute was NOT the look I was trying to attain
with my vessel.

But I did have some adventures on her. My
first sail to Catalina Island was a big deal for me
at the time. It was just far enough away where
you couldn't see it. Back then we relied on
our compass and landmarks. I hadn't mastered
celestial, and wouldn't for years. But I did sail to
Catalina, 26 miles across the channel, and it was
a great adventure for me. I would sail over, drop a
hook, and felt like a real sailor.

Bob, Jim & his Jeet Kun Do Sefu Richard Bustillo on Outlaw

> Chapter 15 <
Bigger Things are to Come.

Anyway, I figured I could do some real cruising! But not in Outlaw. Outlaw was too small. I couldn't even stand up in her and I won't go into the contortions I had to go thru to use the head! I had cleaned her up pretty good and in doing so made her a little more valuable. Over the year I had her I had paid her off free and clear. A good way for a boat to be.

And then I saw my first Formosa. I fell in love. It was a Formosa 41, also known as a Sea Wolf ketch, named Jade Lady. She was the most beautiful boat I had ever seen in King Harbor. Formosas were built at the Formosa Boat Yard by C.Y. Chen in Taipei. She had more class than any boat I had ever seen.

I was hooked. I had to have a Formosa! But they were expensive. I checked, and found that I could have a Formosa 46 or 47 (they were two different designs) for about $85,000 if I bought it in Taiwan and sailed it back to California.

The dream had struck. In the meantime my "other life" went on I still had my motorcycleing life to consider. I know, what has that got to do with anything, right? Well, as it turns out, a lot. You see, we sold a lot of biker goodies thru the magazine and I found that I could get some great prices on biker goodies by going to Taiwan to buy them in quantities. So my new partner in the head shop, Daniel (Patrick had moved on to bigger and better things), and I got tickets to Taipei thru my travel agency, and soon we were on a big silver bird heading to the land of cheap bike stuff and beautiful boats!

As soon as we arrived we took care of the biker stuff, and after ordering a few thousand little biker pins and belt buckles we headed to the Formosa Boat Yard, where we met with C.Y. Chen and his designer. I had pretty much decided on the 46 which had a "saltier" look to it, and my head went nuts trying to figure out how I could buy it. Meanwhile, we also flew down to Taichung where most of the other Taiwan boats were built. We saw a lot we liked, but none like the Formosa. We flew back to Redondo Beach and I put Outlaw up for sale. I didn't know how I would pay for it, but I had to have the Formosa.

And then, as luck would have it, fate stepped in. This was about the time when interest rates went up to 22%. One day I was reading the Log Newspaper, which was the waterfront freebee, and I saw a Formosa 51 for sale. That was a dream boat to me, and the price wasn't too bad. It was owned by three partners and they were always fighting over how the last one left the boat, or didn't fill the tank or whatever, and the interest rates were killing them. It was for sale for $125,000. I wanted it! I couldn't think of anything else. I wanted that boat!

Meanwhile, I wasn't getting any bites on the Newport. But I talked to the owners of the Formosa. They wanted out bad. I wanted in bad. It was a match made in heaven! I offered them $100,000. They came back at me with $110,000. I said okay if they would carry the paper for 3 years and take my Newport in trade. They said no to Outlaw, but they would carry the paper if I gave

Life was starting to change, from biker to sailor

them $10,000 down. I begged, borrowed and…
well, begged and borrowed, and got the $10,000.

We hauled the boat at King Harbor Boat Yard.
During the survey I found some dry rot in one
bulkhead. It gave me an edge. I told the sellers if
they would knock off what the boatyard wanted to
fix the dry rot, I would still go thru with the deal.
They hedged a little, and then gave in.

I knew the guys at the boat yard pretty well.
So I went in and talked to Steve, one of the
owners. I told him I wanted him to give me an
estimate on how much it would cost me to fix the
dry rot, and to do it right. He went out and looked
at it, and said it would cost about $15,000 to pull
that part of the bulkhead and repair the area right
and refinish it with new teak face.

The sellers had a kitten right there in the yard,
but I held my ground. I thought the deal was going
to fall thru, and I was about ready to collapse and
split it with them. Then they had a conference
there in the yard and came back over to where I
was standing.

"Okay, $95,000," they said, "but we still want
the $10,000 down and 22% interest."

I agreed, they agreed, we all agreed, and it
was a done deal. The Formosa 51 was mine!

And so was Outlaw!

There is only one thing dumber than a man
who owns a boat, and that is a man who owns two
boats. If you have three you are just an idiot. Ask
anyone who has been there.

I also had another problem. Where to put it. Slips in King Harbor were harder to find than morals in Congress. I ended up making a deal with the marina. I gave up my 30-foot slip and took a 60-foot end tie. The only way I could do it was to buy the old derelict 27-foot Thunderbird sailboat that was now there sharing the dock. This wasn't difficult. The owner said I could have it for $3,000.

I was now an official idiot! I owned three boats!

I sold the 30-foot Thunderbird to my partner in the head shop with the only provision, being he had to find a slip for it. Now I had a 60-foot slip for the boat but I still had the 30-foot Newport to tie up. At the time there were mooring buoys behind the breakwater and I was able to get one for $175 a quarter. Yeah, really! Things were a lot better then. And about three weeks later Guy Spencer happened along and said he had tried to buy Outlaw from my broker and was told it was sold.

It wasn't! So I sold it to him for $30,000. That was the good news. The bad news was I had to take his grungy old powerboat in trade. It was a liveaboard type boat. Not really safe to go to sea in. So I gave him $10,000 for the old powerboat, he gave me $20,000 (I made a profit!) for the Newport. Then some guy who wanted to live aboard said if I would give him the slip, he would buy the powerboat for $15,000 if I would take payments. I did, and once again I was a one boat owner.

I moved the 51 out onto a mooring ball and went to work making her into what I wanted - a true traditional sailboat. I had learned on Stone Witch that not a lot was needed. This one even had a motor and batteries, and a VHF! How kewl was that? I hadn't even named her yet, but I knew something would hit me so I didn't worry.

The first evening on the mooring I was cleaning up below when I heard the sound of a saxophone wailing outside. I walked up on the deck and it was just at sunset. As it turned out, a liveaboard out on the moorings was a saxophonist. Every evening at sunset he would partake of some righteous bud and wail to the setting sun with some of the best sax music I have ever heard. I was alone on the boat sitting there on the foredeck, leaning back against the mast, listening to the great music and watching the sun set in the west. It could not have been a better day. That night I slept in the boat for the first time.

The next day I rented my house to a friend, and moved aboard. I was home!

> Chapter 16 <
A Rose is a Rose, is a Rose. The Lost Soul is Born.

Back then I was a partner in a small motorcycle parts business where we sold the crap we had bought in Taiwan thru the magazine. Little things like pins, patches and belt buckles. The name of the company was Two Lost Souls. It was named after my old partner, Patrick, and myself. We even had a logo. It was a pennant with "Two Lost Souls" over a figure depicting the Grim Reaper. I flew this pennant high on the top of my main mast.

Anyway, I was having the house I had lived in and had rented out, painted before the new tenant moved in. One day as I was leaving I said I'd be out on the boat, and one of the painters said "You mean on Lost Soul?"

And the name was born. It fit me to a "T." I was truly a lost soul and now I had the perfect name for my boat.

Lost Soul was a Formosa 51 club-footed staysail ketch with a center cockpit and raised poop-deck. That just meant she had two masts and two headsails. The jib was hanked on with brass clips, the staysail the same, and was attached to a teak boom (the club-foot) so it was easy to single-hand her.

Above decks there was a lot of teak. I kept the teak decks natural, but bleached them twice a year and washed them down with saltwater at least once a month to keep them looking that beautiful honey color.

Some people would consider the varnished areas above deck a bad thing as you need to keep up with teak to stay looking new. I loved it. I enjoyed it when I would varnish every couple months. I had to build the varnish until I had at least 8 coats on her. So each time I varnished I would add two coats. Once the base was set, each coat went on easier and the boat shined!

The masts were boxed teak and looked great. But I have to admit varnishing them was tough. Once they were varnished they looked great!

On the aft deck, which was all teak, was a teak box that held a lot of the little things we need at hand. The top of the box had a pad on it which I had covered in a gray Sunbrella so it wasn't so hot when you would sit or lay on it.

Below decks she was perfect with teak bulkheads highly varnished as well as teak and holly cabin soles. Lots of teak cabinetry, and teak doors with sailing ships carved into them. The layout couldn't have been better.

Look at the logo on the t-shirt. Two Lost Souls is where the name for Lost Soul originated.

One of the first things I did was to paint all the blue areas black. Then I had all the blue canvas replaced with black canvas.

She was a classic! A staysail ketch with teak decks and hank-on sails. The sails were old, but serviceable. I had the name painted by a local artist and she copied the artwork from Pirates of the Caribbean (the ride… this was long before the picture!)

It didn't take long for me to get Lost Soul #1 (this was the first of two boats I would name Lost Soul) looking the way I wanted her. Every day I would come back to her after working a half-day at the magazine and a half-day at Hermosa High, the head shop. I worked on polishing the hull, learned how to varnish and turned the old wood rails and massive bright-work areas of the topside into the rich, beautiful color only varnish can bring out in teak. It was a lot of work, but every time I would approach the boat I fell in love with the boat all over again.

At the time I had a pet I had brought out to the boat to live with me. It was a 12-foot, 80-pound Burmese python named Worm. My friend Billy Jack had given her to me when she was less than a foot long and I had raised her. She was too big to fit in a terrarium, so I let her roam the boat. I figured I would not have any problem with rats. Once a week I would pop a "feeder rabbit" into the forward porthole. She was a happy snake. I was also the only boat on the moorings that didn't have a seagull or pelican problem. Even though we were on a mooring just 50 feet from the bait barge, birds seemed to avoid my boat as if it had the plague… or a snake on it! Lol.

Her favorite place to "hang out" was on top of the main boom,which had a black sail cover on it. That drew in the heat and she loved it up there. Plenty of fishermen in their dinghies who would be fishing nearby would get quite a start when they would think she was a rubber snake, which some boaters use to try and keep birds off their boat. Only thing was, this one moved! When I'd come home and crawl into my bunk she would hear me and come out from wherever she was staying warm and curl up next to me to get some body heat.

Okay, now I know there are a buncha folks going "are you friggin' nuts? Living with a dangerous snake aboard? Okay, so once again

I must move a little off subject to give you an
insight into raising snakes, or any kind of large
animal that can eat you. When Billy Jack gave me
Worm she was less than a foot long. She was a
baby. Now most people, when they have a small
reptile, keep it in a terrarium. It's like a fish tank
with gravel in it. I was no exception. Otherwise I
would have woken up in the middle of the night
on my meander to the head and hear crunch
underfoot. Not something I'd want to do. So when
it comes time to feed said reptile most folks open
the top of the terrarium and drop in whatever
fresh goodies they might be feeding them. When
they are real small that would be crickets. What
I would do everyday when I would get home, I
would open the terrarium and lift Worm out. I
would play with her. Let her squirm around my
desk, or while I would watch TV let her snuggle
in where it was warm. Usually next to my butt or
in my lap were her favorites. When it was feeding
day, while she was out of her terrarium, I would
drop the food in. When she would "go home"
every once and awhile she'd find a tasty treat.
That way she never associated the opening of the
terrarium with food. Those that are used to only
seeing the top open when there is food usually
snap at whatever comes into their home when the
lid opens. Worm never learned that. Over the 15
years I owned her, whenever I would come home,
no matter the time, I would take her out of her
home and play with her. After awhile, when she'd

reached 5-6 feet, I didn't keep her in the terrarium any more. I kept the top off, but left the heat lamp on inside. By then she was eating mice, and then rats. I would just drop the "food" in while she was out of the terrarium, and she would find it soon enough. By the time I moved her onto the boat she didn't need a terrarium any more.

All the years I had her she never once snapped at or tried to bite anyone. She was the perfect boat pet. When she "did her business" it was a nice neat little package that could just be dropped over the side. The fish loved it!

Okay, back to reality! The boat life.

One of the first things I wanted to do when I got Lost Soul was to sail over to Catalina's back side. That had always seemed to be where "the cruisers" went and I'd always been intimidated about going there. On the east side there were moorings and ship to shore boats, but on the Cat Harbor side, even though there were moorings, they also had room to anchor and I wanted to get some experience anchoring.

Now here comes the funny part. So I gathered a crew consisting of a good friend of mine and a couple young ladies, and we sailed off to Catalina for the weekend. We left Friday in the afternoon and got in just before sunset. Perfect timing. I checked out the anchorage and it wasn't too crowded, so I headed over to a spot that looked good with no other boats around and when I had the hook where I wanted it, I told Bruce to let it go and started backing towards the shore.

It wasn't more than a minute when Bruce yelled out, "Hey, there's only about 10 feet of chain on this!" And then it hit me, I didn't even check the chain and rode. The anchor sat in the chocks, had chain attached, and I "assumed" everything was fine.

So here we come to Rule #2. Never assume!

I put the boat in neutral and ran below as fast as I could, and forward to the anchor locker. There I found my worst fears come true. There was less than 100 feet of anchor rode and the bitter end was not attached. I quickly tied the bitter end to the Sampson post that ran down thru the anchor locker and ran back on deck.

"How much do you think we have out so far?" I asked Bruce.

"Maybe 30-40 feet," he replied.

I looked at the depth sounder and it said we were sitting in about 25 feet of water. I made a quick decision and told him to go ahead and drop the rest as I put her into reverse to back down on the anchor. Little did I know that there was a cluster of rocks just behind me. I found that out a few seconds later when the depth sounder went from 20 feet to --- feet (that's no reading!) and I felt the rudder hit a rock.

By now the audience (that'd be everyone who was already anchored and knew there were rocks there!) was having a wonderful afternoon watching the idiot bikers try to anchor. I can remember distinctly thinking that someday I would be experienced enough to know to check the chart prior to dropping the hook, and I couldn't wait for that day to come.

You will never have enough experience to know everything. This was pounded home to me almost 15 years later, when Jody and I sailed back to Cat Harbor on the boat we had sailed all over the world on. We were definitely experienced! That trip had covered many years and about 75,000 miles. And I dropped my hook and backed into the very same pile of rocks!!

But back to the time line!

I told Bruce to bring the anchor back aboard (we had an electric windlass, so that wasn't too bad) and tried to look like I knew what I was doing for the ladies we'd conned into going "yachting" for the weekend. We anchored in about 30 feet in sand and felt the hook grab. Yeah, I know. At least 5-1 for chain and 7-1 for rode. But I didn't know that at that time.

But wait, there's more! We dinghied ashore and walked across the isthmus to Doug's Harbor Reef, the bar that was located at the Isthmus between Two Harbors and Catalina Harbor. After we'd had a few coldies to settle our nerves we made our way back to the boat to see what kind of fun we could find to do on the boat. We did, indeed, find a way to have fun. And after about a half bottle of tequila shooters we found our way to our bunks to play some adult games!

Somewhere around 4:00 a.m. I awoke and felt the need to visit the head. Not wanting to bother using the head, I walked out onto the deck, still in a state of half-sleep, dropped trou and proceeded to see how deep the water was (that's a joke!). As I stood there feeling the relief of emptying my bladder I started to look around. It was beautiful. Not a cloud in the sky. The water was as smooth as glass, and the most beautiful part of it all was how quiet and peaceful it was being out at sea.

Er, out at sea? Wait a minute. We were supposed to be snuggly anchored in Cat Harbor.

As I started to come out of my stupor and looked around, we were about a mile offshore. I walked to the bow and the anchor line hung straight down!

I remember sitting down on the aft deck box and just looking at where we had been anchored. I honestly did not want to go below and wake anyone. That would let them know what a total dunderhead they had in charge of the boat. But there was no way out of it.

I went down below and roused Bruce from a dead sleep, and checked out the hottie next to him while I was at it (Hey, I like girls!!). He came up on deck and looked around. Then he looked at me, and the look on his face was as close to the Mona Lisa smile than I had ever seen.

Suffice it to say, over the next few months 400 feet of 3/8" chain was added to our anchor locker.

> Chapter 17 <
Living the Life of a Cruiser for the First Time!

I, like many others, wanted to cruise but had to earn a living. I have noticed that life often gets in the way of living. By time I was editor of Choppers Magazine and Big Bike Magazine. In my spare time I was also publishing a tabloid for the outlaw biker community called FTW Newsmagazine (don't ask!). That, in itself, was pretty funny because I'd quit High School to join the service when I was 17. I needed an editor to edit what I wrote. I did go back to college when I got out of the service, but by then the damage was done. I learned that I was good at telling stories, but my use of the English language was atrocious. Of course, sitting here now, having just passed my 71st birthday, I also see that it didn't matter all that much. Over 1,200 magazine articles in a dozen assorted titles, and this being my 8th book, I guess I fooled everyone. Even you!

But back then the good news was I had Degenerate Jim working with me, and he had a degree in English Lit. So I was covered. But I also had my head shop, gym, martial arts supply outlet and travel agency. You'd think I was in the money, but actually I was just a workaholic and liked to stay busy. Still am.

But now I had my boat. I wanted to go cruising.

It took a few months but I managed to off-load the travel agency to my partner in that endeavor, and sold the gym to a nice elementary school teacher (and had to carry the paper on it), and talked Degenerate Jim into handling the magazines while I would go sailing for three weeks. The plan was that I would fly home to work on them to get them all out by deadline.

Preparing for the voyage was unbelievable, and I still think it is the best part of any voyage. In the planning all things are perfect. I would make weekly trips to San Pedro, to a small shop where the shipping companies purchased their charts and cruising guides of the world. It was called Southwest Instruments, and it has long since gone out of business. But back then it was a cruiser's dream. It was a small storefront just off the harbor. For those of you not familiar with San Pedro, it has been a commercial harbor since the early 1800s. The store on the street level had a repair facility that repaired ship's compasses, sextants, RDFs (Radio Direction Finders) and other instruments of the day.

Ah, but down in the basement. That was

where dreams were made. The whole basement was filled with hanging paper charts. Different bins held different areas of the world. Wandering thru the basement of Southwest Instruments could turn any grown man who is a cruiser into a little boy again, and I was no exception.

The lady that ran that area was very friendly and knew more about sailing routes of the world than anyone I have met since. As we were planning to just head south to Cabo she herded us over to the Mexico bin. There we found overall charts to plan the voyage, and then individual charts of all of the anchorages along the way. She told us we should also have charts of anywhere we might have to pull into in an emergency, and then sent us upstairs to find the right cruising guides for the time.

Rule #8. Always have paper charts on board when you are cruising. All the new electronics are well and good, but if and when they stop working, you will still have a mark on a chart letting you know where you are.

I can remember twice on our world cruise when we lost our electronic navigation. Once when our batteries died and our generator wouldn't start we were without power for a full day, and we were offshore in the Hawaiian Islands. We did managed to charge the batteries with an emergency little Honda generator we had stored on the boat just for that purpose, but to get our 3500-amp batteries up to 11 volts, the minimum they would work at, took a long time! The second time we did a accidental jibe and the sheet line popped the Loran antenna off in mid Atlantic. We managed to get in with our paper charts.

But back to planning our Mexico voyage. Then, as it is today, Charlie's Charts was the bible for that trip. So we picked up a fresh copy, along with the Coastal Pilots by the U.S. Government, which at that time were less than $10 each. That night I dreamed the voyage over and over. I went over the overall chart using my new calipers to measure how many miles it was from port to port, and I lived the voyage in advance.

My first trip would be down the Baja to Cabo San Lucas. By then it had been a few years since I'd been there. It was a 700-mile sail, and instead of doing it like we did on Stone Witch, which was due south and then due east until we hit it, I opted to stay just offshore and stop a few times. I had three weeks to do it in, so I had plenty of time.

I had a biker friend named Rat who was a diesel mechanic and he offered to go thru my engine. That was something I really wanted done, and for the next couple weeks he stayed on the boat and got the diesel in tip-top shape. When he finished he told me he was shipping his bike to Hawaii, and if I ever sailed there to look him up. I said I would try.

My crew for this trip was a young lady I had met who liked sailing, Bruce, a bodybuilder that worked out and helped run my gym, and his girlfriend. We had a crew of four!

First stop was in San Diego just before Halloween. Halloween was a big thing for cruisers in San Diego because the insurance companies wouldn't cover damages if you sailed south before November 1. So October 31st was the big party. It was thrown by PMS (that's Pacific Marine supply.) During the early '80s they would have a huge bash on Halloween with hot dogs, specials on cruiser's stuff, and it was a big deal.

On the morning of November 1st we all headed south. The Pacific Trades blow down the coast, as does the Eastern Pacific current, so it is usually a milk-run. The first time I went down was no exception. Our first run was about 150 miles to Isla San Martine. It was a sleepy village on a small island, but to us it was our first foreign port. It was also my first overnight passage since Stone Witch and the first one where I was the skipper.

Back then we had a ritual on board Lost Soul. At sunset we would have a "sunset joint." (This was long before 'zero tolerance.') We would roll a fatty and enjoy the setting of the sun with the stereo playing rock and roll. After that we'd have some dinner and play a VHS video, with whoever was on watch sitting in the companionway, checking the horizon every five minutes.

Here was where I learned Rule #1 of cruising. NEVER arrive at a strange anchorage at night. Do whatever you can to arrive in daylight hours.

We didn't. We'd come in late at night. Back

then I couldn't afford radar, Loran,, GPS,or
Satellite navigation which were only for the
very rich. We dropped our sails 3 miles out,
when we could see the small lights of the village
(navigation buoys were not very dependable
in Mexico back then) and we slowly motored
towards what looked like a good anchorage on our
charts. As soon as the depth sounder said 50 feet
we dropped our hook and anchored just off the
small beach where the fishing pangas were.

In the morning we watched them take off
for the day's fishing, and then we hoisted our
hook and headed a little over 10 miles south to a
beautiful little bay that was protected by a large
"hooked" peninsula called San Quintine. This was
a paradise. We anchored in 17 feet of water that
was so clear you could see the anchor set. It was
like glass. There was a small river that we took the
dinghy up, and we spent the day hanging out on
the boat. The water was still too cool for serious
swimming. You see, the Alaskan current is what
pushes the Eastern Pacific current, and just as the
Gulf Stream brings warm waters north from the
Caribbean, the Eastern Pacific current brings cold
water south to the Baja.

Having learned rule #1, we hung out the
next day so we could depart at sunset for our
next anchorage, Islas San Benito. It was about
125 miles and most of it would be offshore, as
the shoreline tucked in. The only danger was the
Sacramento Reef reef, about four miles off San

Antonio point, roughly35 miles south. We would pass it while it was still dark out, so we swung a little to the west to give it good clearance. It used to eat about 1-2 boats a year.

It all went perfect. We arrived well before sunset at the three small islands that made up Islas San Benito. Before we even had the anchor set we were approached by a couple of fishermen who had a tent on the beach ashore. As it turned out, they were actually lobster fishermen. It didn't take long before they were headed ashore to their camp with a six-pack of ice cold Coors and two copies of Penthouse, and we were down below giving four lobsters a hot bath!

I won't bore you with the rest of the trip, but it was everything I had hoped it would be and more. We covered the next 500 miles in a week, stopping a couple times along the way, and then a three-day, two-night passage into Cabo San Lucas. The changes in just a few short years were hard to believe. A small marina had been built inside, and there were now a couple hotels on the beach. The road thru town had been paved! It was unbelievable!

Once you rounded Cabo Falso and came into Cabo San Lucas the water warmed considerably. The water that came down from the Sea of Cortez was warm, and it curved around the point and into the beach area. We anchored pretty much where we had anchored on the Witch, and I had a few days to "hang out" before I had to fly home and work.

The plan had worked. When I flew into LAX Jim picked me up and we had everything we needed to do completed in plenty of time. I had found my way to escape!

> Chapter 18 <
A New Challenge, a Big Storm,
and a Big Adventure Begins.

Over the next few years I made the trip down
to Mexico about every other year. Each time
I sailed further, once down to Puerto Vallarta
on the mainland, and once all the way down to
Zihuatanejo. Each time I would fly home every
three weeks for a week, and then fly back down to
either continue the voyage south or sail the boat
back up to Redondo.

Soon it lost its adventure. I needed more
to get my juices flowing. Hawaii! Twenty-six
hundred nautical miles to Paradise. That was it.

Once again I spent a lot of time at Southwest
Instruments picking up all the charts, including
the overall chart of the Pacific (which hangs today
in my office with every path I have sailed on it
marked well!). But there was more. I studied
everything that I could find on cruising. You see,
back then (this was the '80s and will probably
sound funny) the common wisdom was to tear off

the labels from the cans and mark what's in them with a magic marker, so when they get wet and the label falls off you will know what's in them. And to varnish (no kidding!) your eggs, so they will last longer.

A good friend, Dr. Larry Hazen was getting ready to take off on a Pacific voyage, so he was the one we would all go to for the best cruising advice. Being a doctor (he was a podiatrist) he had dozens of those plastic IV bottles they use in hospitals. They were perfect for storing spices, oil and God knows what else. Everything in his boat was stored that way.

The medical kit and what was in it was also a full time job. First you had to find a doctor to put all of the stuff you'd need in it. Then you had to be sure you knew how to cut off a limb and sew it up! I won't say we went overboard, as it is very important to know what to do in an emergency, but it's a lot easier today with SSB radios and GPS and such. But anyone sailing offshore for more than a week at a time should at least know how to suture a wound.

Oh, yeah. And then there was navigating across an ocean. This was a major. I couldn't afford a Sat-Nav or a weather-fax or a Single-Sideband radio. That stuff was well out of my budget. No, I was going to have to learn how to navigate using celestial navigation. That mean using a sextant! Now let me tell you. My mind was not created for the sextant. I bought a decent

used sextant at Southwest Instruments and the
books that went with it. I studied all the diagrams
and math, and looked at all the reference tables
and did all the things that mariners of the time did.
But in the end I could not figure out how to locate
where I was standing on Earth without looking
around me. And I knew that looking around when
in mid ocean would not help much.

My neighbor in the marina was an old salt
named Bill Larson who lived on a 41' square-
rigged ketch. It was salty and so was he. In fact,
he had added a square-sail on the top of his main
mast. Many years later he would skipper the Lady
Washington tall ship! So I asked him to teach me.
We went down below on his boat and he started
talking about angles and variation and deviation
(I knew how to be a deviate!!) and all kinds of
things. None of which I understood at all.

As the day to depart grew near I was pretty
worried. I did not know how to figure my position
using a sextant.

And then it happened. Being a prudent
mariner (hah!) I decided I should have a backup sextant. Just in case. Then, as now, whatever
you have as a backup means the original will not
break! So off to Southwest Instruments again, and
I bought a $25 (yes, that's how much they were
then!) plastic Davis sextant. It came in a neat little
plastic case, with a neat little booklet about 15
pages long... telling you how to use it!!!

And I understood it immediately! There were

two little paragraphs telling me how to take a noon site. That would be all I'd need. If I knew where I was each day at noon, I could navigate anywhere on earth!

And so it was on the 13th of November (it was a Friday too!) 1981, I took off to sail to Hawaii. The crew for this voyage was Lindy, the girl I was going with at the time. She was a redhead from Wisconsin and at 19 had quit her job at Hermosa Gift and decided to have an adventure. Her girlfriend decided to come as well. Bruce, the bodybuilder from my gym, rounded out the crew.

I planned a break-in cruise down to Cabo. By

Lost Soul anchred in Two Harbrs, Catalina

now that was like my second home and it was a perfect "jumping off point" for the crossing, as it is located at 22.5° north and Hawaii is at 20°. The sail down to Cabo was where I tested my skills with the sextant, and by the time we reached our destination there I felt I was proficient enough. I took a noon- site each day and marked it on my chart. I then did a dead-reckoning position based on either landmarks I could sea, or on the speed and course as entered in the ship's log every two hours by the person coming off watch. All was good.

We arrived in Cabo just before the first of December and dropped our hook like we always did. It was much more crowded then it had been in previous years, as cruising was starting to explode with the decent economy. I found a spot next to a Force 50 owned by Joe Picus, and we did the Cabo Drop: Let out 150' of chain and back to the beach. The hook grabbed and with the motor in reverse we were about 10 feet off the beach when Bruce jumped in and took the stern anchor up onto the beach. We were set. We decided to hang out for a week or so before jumping off for the islands. The town was hopping and the weather was perfect.

The morning of December 8th has since gone down in cruising history. Being an early riser, I had taken my crew ashore for breakfast early, and about 8:00 a.m. we were returning to the boat just as Joe Picus and his crew were leaving for breakfast. Bernard Moitessier, a well know French sailor and author, was also anchored nearby. As I recall (because sometimes things that long ago get fuzzy, and I don't want to make a mistake here), there was a little wind starting to kick up, but it wasn't bad. There were no breakers on the beach where we were anchored.

I went below to work on a book I was writing and was pretty deep in thought. I felt the boat starting to move a little just before Bruce yelled from up on deck.

"Bob, you need to come out here and take a look at this!"

I climbed up the companionway ladder and when I got on deck looked at the sky. It had become very dark. VERY dark. And there were white caps about a mile offshore, heading in our direction.

"You're right," I said to Bruce. "This doesn't look good."

As it turned out, this was the understatement of the decade.

The girls were on the foredeck laying out to get a little sun before it got too hot, as it had been the last couple days. In a matter of minutes the white caps had moved over half the distance from the point of land that marks the end of the Baja Peninsula to where we were anchored, and all of a sudden we were starting to get swells and small waves. Waves can only happen in water that is as deep as half their wave-length. The fast drop off at Cabo went from 1 foot to 100 feet in about 100 feet. It was very steep. That was why we anchored the way we did.

I told Bruce to grab the stern hook, but before he could get it a swell picked the boat up at the bow and it pulled towards shore. At the time our rudder was only a few feet from the sand.

"Forget the stern-hook," I yelled at him, "Go stand by the windlass and prepare to haul the anchor." I turned and un-cleated the 50-foot line that was holding our 35-lb. Bruce stern hook with 20 feet of chain and flung it onto the beach. "Start hauling the anchor," I said, and the girls went forward with him to help flake the chain as I fired up the Ford Lehman 135hp diesel. It fired right up and I threw it into gear just as a large wave broke on the bow, picking it up and turning us to starboard about 25°. I put the RPMs up to 2,000 (we normally ran her at 1,500) and felt the rudder slightly touch the sand as we started to move forward. It was a good thing we had been thrown to starboard, as Joe's Force 50 was only about 15 feet away from us on the port. And no one was on board her, as they'd gone to breakfast.

I looked forward and saw Bruce was pulling the chain in and then heard the anchor go "clunk" and lock into its chock. When they all got back to the aft cockpit and were safe I looked back at the beach and it was a disaster. Everything was moving like slow motion. I saw the Force 50 rear up, pulling its anchor line like a horse rearing up, and then the boat fell on its side on the beach.

Waves started to crash into her, pushing her further up the beach. The winds were up over 60 knots by then, from an almost calm morning. I had never seen or heard of anything like it.

Looking at the direction of the wind, all I wanted to do was to get to a lee shore. The wind direction was onshore, but it was clocking pretty fast. Before the freak storm ended 27 boats wound up on the beach, including Moitessier's famous boat, Joshua.

I honestly don't remember how long we motored around outside the bay. Looking back it only seems like less than a day. Soon the winds clocked around and were coming offshore. We motored back into the bay and dropped our hook about10 feet off the beach. The wind was blowing at about 55 knots right off the sandy beach. I then let out about 100 feet of chain. At that point I shackled another 65-lb. Danforth I had as a spare and let out another 100 feet. I added my last spare anchor, a 90-lb. old Fisherman anchor I'd bought at a marine swap meet and thought I'd never use, and then let out the balance of the chain, for a total length of 400 feet with three anchors. It held.

The wind blew for quite awhile longer, but it did subside. The following day it was as if it had never happened except for the boats on the beach. This is where the cruisers came together. Everyone worked at getting the closest boat to the water back into the water. They dug out the sand, ran lines out to fishing boats and dinghies and whatever else could pull. After a few days (I honestly don't remember how many!) we'd gotten more than half the boats launched. I think we launched 11. And then the Mexican government said we had until Saturday to get whatever boats we could launched. After that they would push them up the beach into Doc Ross's salvage yard with their bulldozers.

A week later you would not know it ever happened.

I remember meeting Lin and Larry Pardey there, after the storm. It was the first time I met them in person, and they were (and still are) gods to me. But now, almost 35 years later, we are also old friends!

After about 5 days of helping get the boats off the beach we all watched as the Mexican government brought in the bulldozer and mashed the remaining boats up the beach. It was a somber time, and we wanted to head out for some more adventure.

> Chapter 19 <
Westbound and Down! A Real Test
for My Navigational Skills.

We listened to the VHF the following morning to see how the winds off Cabo Falso were. The fishing boats would go out very early and then they'd report in for any sailboats that were heading out around the point and northbound. We weren't northbound, but it was good to know the winds were not howling around the point.

Once again it was the 13th when we departed. This time the 13th of December. This time it was a Monday.

We sailed out of Cabo San Lucas and bid adieu to land for the foreseeable future. I have to tell you, I was as nervous as a virgin at his first orgy! I had three other people whose lives were in my hands.

According to the British Admiralty's Ocean Passages the best way to Hawaii was to sail a little southwest, and then turn slowly more westerly as the trades filled in. Or, as cruisers would put it, sail south until the butter melts, then turn west until you hear the ukuleles. Ocean Passages was a compilation by the British Admiralty's over 100 years experiences of sailing ships. Before Jimmy Cornell wrote World Cruising Routes, this was the bible for sailing ships. It took me many years to realize that although these were good routes, they had been created for square-rigged ships. Square-rigged ships sail best downwind. Modern Marconi-rigged sailboats sail better just off the wind. But more on that later.

The first day we watched the land disappear behind us. Slowly Cabo faded, and as the sun set, and we had our Sunset Joint and the final lights were gone. We were "out at sea." I have a hard time describing the feeling of losing the sight of land the first time when you are the Captain. It is a mixture of adventure, fear and freedom. The adventure of crossing an ocean. The fear that you may not be able to find that little dot on the chart that says Hawaiian Islands, and the freedom that you are in charge of your own destiny.

My watch was going to be the 2:00 to 4:00 a.m. watch. We took 2 hour watches. This meant that the watch schedule would constantly change so no one got stuck with a bad shift all the time. I would have the 2:00 to 4:00 a.m. watch, then the 10:00 to noon watch, then the 6:00 to 8:00 am...

I went below to try and get some sleep and laid in my bunk. And then it hit me. The paranoia.

Anyone familiar with smoking pot can tell you there are times it does create paranoia. All I could think of as I laid in my bunk was I had 3 people and myself who's lives were in my hands. What if we didn't find land? What if we missed the islands? How far would we have to sail before hitting Japan, China, or God knows where?

It was during this two- to three-hour bit of paranoia that I decided I would no longer partake of the Sunset Joint. I didn't know it at the time, but it was probably that night that saved my life. Many of my friends who never did stop, well, let's just say that drugs never did any of them any good.

Okay, I am off the soap box now. On with the

Setting off across the Pacific.. Aaaagh!

voyage.

Every day, about mid day, I would break out the sextant. I had gotten so used to taking a noon site to get my longitude I could almost do it in my head. I'd take a few sightings starting a few minutes before noon on my watch, and when the sun reached its highest point (technically the zenith) mark the time. Then all I had to do was convert the time to GMT (Greenwich Mean Time) as this was before they started calling it Universal Time or Zulu. After that it was a no brainer. Just figure out how many minutes you were from Greenwich at high noon, and each minute equaled 60 nautical miles. Very roughly this would tell you how far you are from 0°. All I needed to do after that was add the declination from the tables provided in a little book, and viola! There we were.

So each day I would studiously take a noon site and mark it on the chart, including the date, with a pencil. At the same time, as a backup, I would also mark our dead-reckoning position. This I got by taking the average speed over the previous 24 hours, and the average course steered, and place a small red "X" with the date. This was because we were extremely fastidious about keeping the ship's log. I can't emphasize how important that log would turn out to be on many occasions.

So each person, after their watch, would put the date, time, their name, the approximate speed,

approximate course, a weather note and then any
silly little thing they wanted to ad in the note
section. This would give me the average speed and
course. But something weird was happening. The
third day out I started to worry. The red "X" was
getting further and further behind the pencil "X". I
figured this was due to a current or something that
I didn't understand, and felt pretty good we were
making such great time.

You see, I had decided before we left that I
would not use the RDF (Radio Direction Finder)
and do it the way "real sailors" had done it for
hundreds of years. I figured I had to be as smart as
they were, right? The 8th day out I found out that
was not exactly correct. You see, 8 days out we
saw a tanker way off on the horizon. Being excited
to see a boat, we jumped on the VHF radio and
called them. The boat was the Bass Pike, an oil
tanker out heading around the horn. This was most
kewl to all of us.

"Can you give me a position?" I asked. I
wanted to verify where we were with someone
who knew what they were doing.

"Sure mate, no problem," came the reply, "We
just had this new system installed. It's a Satellite
Navigation System and I can actually tell you your
position, course and speed!" He was almost as
excited as I was.

"You are on a 250° heading doing 5.4 knots,
and your position is exactly..." and at this point
he gave me our Lat & Long down to the double

decimal point. I thanked him and after we signed off I grabbed the chart to put down our position for the first time in ink.

Oops! If his position was correct we were hundreds of miles behind where I thought we were. In fact, we were just a tad behind where the red Xs were.

Now I had a quandary. I didn't want to tell my crew what a friggin' idiot I was, but how could I not? But first I had to figure out what I had done wrong. I went over my figures a dozen times: the time of high noon at our location, distance from GMT at their noon, add the declination.. and...

About the fifth time I re-figured it I found my mistake. It seems that while we had sat in Cabo San Lucas enjoying the storm and all, the declination changed from adding it to subtracting it. So each day, as the declination increased, instead of subtracting it I added it. This compounded the distance, so each day I was adding more and more distance that I should have been subtracting. I did what I had to do and told the crew. I have to tell you I took more than a little hazing, but at last I was getting good and true readings.

The voyage to Hawaii from Cabo is about 2,300 miles as the crow flies. We, of course, were not crows. We had made some southing as suggested by the Admiralty and were now on a due west heading. All was going well. On the 21st day I figured we were only about 100 miles out.

Life was good and the boat was handling great. What could go wrong?

Rule #3. Never ask ,"What could go wrong?" as it will.

Around 3:00 in the afternoon I glanced up at the rigging and saw something no sailor wants to see. Our port upper spreader was hanging as limp as a pecker on Sunday morning. The shroud that was to hold it place was still attached to the end of it with the sail tape we added to keep any chafe from happening, but the other end was no longer connected to the mast.

We loaded Bruce into the Bosun's Chair and hoisted him up. This is no easy feat when you are at sea, but we had to do it. Soon he had assessed the damage as he was tossed around and beat up by everything that was around him. The thru bolt that held it to the mast had sheared on the port side. The longer part of the bolt, the one that held the starboard spreader in place, was still there, but it was sheared right where it exited the mast on the port side. Rust had done its job.

Now I don't know about you, but we didn't carry any 18" inch long ¾" bolts in our spares.

We finally came up with a Mickey Mouse way to make do. We took down the main and put the storm trysail up in its place. It came to just under the location of that spreader. Then Bruce wrapped some 3/8" line around the mast to hold the starboard spreader in place.

The reason we'd put the storm trisail up was

in case we hit any weather it would not overpower us. That way we could still sail on a port tack without over-stressing the rig. But we would not be able to lower the sail, or would we be able to sail to starboard.

So far so good. We were close to the island. What could go wrong?

Oops, forgot rule #3, didn't I?

A little while later we learned exactly what it was that could go wrong. About 11:00 p.m. the wind started to kick up, but not like the trades which had been running 20-25 knots from behind us. All of a sudden they were clocking around, and soon we were pulling in our sails and trying to motor into a 25-to 30-knot wind right out of the west.

As the wind increased the seas increased and I was getting worried we would not have the fuel to make it if we kept motoring. So we hanked on a storm jib and thanked God we'd put the storm trysail on the main. We left the staysail and mizzen down and battened down everything on deck. This included, but was not limited to a half dozen 5-gallon fuel jugs and the same number of 5-gallon water jugs. Back then you always planned for the worst.

I guess Rule #4, as if you needed it, would be, "Prepare for the worst and hope for the best."

So in a few hours we were being blasted by a 35-knot headwind (they call it a Kona Storm we found out later) and it was blowing us backwards.

With the storm jib and trysail we could barley hold a 60° point of sail, so we were basically moving away from the island for the day and a half of the storm, on a port tack.

But wait! We aren't thru having fun yet. About midnight the next night (why dos this shit always happen at midnight?) we heard a loud bang. I was on watch, and looked thru the dark and could see the storm jib was thrashing about like a bed sheet in a hurricane. I followed the sheet to where it was tied and saw that the strain had not only pulled the car that it was attached to on the track loose, but the track itself had pulled up the boat's teak rail it was attached to.

Now this is not a good thing to have happen in a storm, at night, in heavy seas, in the rain. I called Bruce up on deck and let the autopilot hold the boat on course as we tried to catch the end of the broken rail. It was thrashing about and very dangerous. After a number of tries we were able to lasso it, but not before it whipped around behind the boat and smashed one of the aft windowpanes. Lost Soul had crescent-shaped windows on the stern, held in place by solid brass cross members. The broken rail and track had somehow managed to whip around and shatter the upper corner pane of glass.

We got the flailing piece of teak and rail tied down and retied and routed the storm jib sheet thru a block attached to a deck-mounted cleat. The shattered window pane was well above the water, at least 5 feet, so we figured we'd worry about it in the daylight, as I didn't want anyone hanging upside down off the stern at night in a storm.

By morning the storm had subsided and we were actually becalmed. We wiped down the shattered aft window pane with acetone and then applied a whole large tube of silicone over it. It was waterproof, for sure.

I had not taken a position sighting in two days and had no idea how far off course we were due to the storm. Just about noon the sky cleared and I was able to get a good noon sight. We had sailed north almost 100 miles in two and a half days!

As we were becalmed I calculated our fuel, took an actual measurement of the tanks (opened the floorboards and put a long stick into the tank!) and figured we could probably motor to Hilo, where we planned on clearing in at Radio Bay.

The calm held and we motored for two days. I took a noon sight on the third day and it said we should be about 30 miles off of the Big Island of Hawaii. But we couldn't see it. And it looked clear out. Now, the Big Island of Hawaii has a couple of 13,000 foot peaks called Mauna Kea and Mauna Loa that should have been visible for 100 miles!

We kept motoring in the direction I thought the island should be, and finally I decided that discretion was better than valor. I decided to go ahead and take out the RDF. This was a hard decision, as I really wanted to do it the old-fashioned way. Of course, in today's standards, I guess I did do it the old fashioned way, using an RDF.

For those of you who are unfamiliar with the RDF, it is so simple even an idiot can do it. (Hey ma! He means me!) I brought it up on deck as the crew gathered around. We put in the new batteries we had bought for its use and turned it on. Then we started to rotate the antenna on top. Pretty soon we heard music! And it was pretty clear. We listened for a few minutes and then the disc jockey said the name of the station, and that they were in Lahaina! Bitchin! I drew a line on the chart in the direction of Lahaina using the direction set by the RDF.

Then we started to rotate the antenna again. Viola. In just a few seconds we had a strong signal. We listened until, once again, they said the call letters of the station and that they were broadcasting from Hilo! Real bitchin! That's where we wanted to go! I took the ruler and drew a line on the compass heading the RDF said the station was located. The point where the two lines intersected should have been where we were, exactly.

But wait… according to this we were less than 3 miles off the coast of Hilo? Three miles, no clouds in the sky, and no Hilo? What's up with that?

I started to get worried and asked Bruce to go forward on the bow pulpit and keep an eye out for any sign of land. I was nervous. You can imagine.

My first Pacific crossing, and now this!

It wasn't too long before I heard Bruce from the bow. "Hey bob, check this out! There's a water skier behind a speedboat!"

I looked and sure enough, there was an old Chris Craft speedboat pulling a water skier, and they were heading right for us. As they sped by I shouted at them, "Hey! How far is it to Hilo Bay?!"

They passed by and made a wide turn. Coming back by us the man in the boat pointed straight ahead and said, "About two miles, that way!"

Not a minute later Bruce yelled back to me, " Land-Ho!"

Sure enough, I could see surf breaking on a beach, but nothing beyond it.

When we finally tied up at the Customs Dock in front of the Coast Guard office we learned what happened. It seems that while we were out to sea, about a week earlier, the Kilauea volcano had erupted. That caused a hazy condition due to the small particles of ash that had gone into the air, and the still breeze let it fall so it caused a gray-out. In Hawaii they call it Vog. Visibility was less than 2 miles, unless you were looking up at the sun, as I was, when I took our noon site!

We made it!

> Chapter 20 <
Bad Boys, Bad Boys, Whatcha Gonna Do?

As soon as we tied up I went to the Harbor Master's office to clear in. A little later he came out to the boat for final clearance. I had my guns out and on the aft bunk, unloaded and open. I usually carry a 12-gauge shotgun, the Winchester Police special with a pistol grip and 18 ½" barrel which holds 9 shells Also a .45 that I had custom built many years before, when I was working with Knievel. The Customs man noted them on his report, checked the rest of the boat, and we were all set.

Or so we thought!

The next day I was on a flight to LAX to go back and get an issue of the magazines out. I had set up with Bruce to call me every day at about 2:00 p.m. his time, and told him I'd see him an about a week.

Once back in harness I settled in to get the magazines out on time. Each day I would get a call from Bruce, and in the meantime my lawyer and his wife, with their newborn baby, had flown to Hawaii and were staying on the boat too.

Then one day the phone call didn't come. After a couple hours I called the Coast Guard Station we had tied Lost Soul up in front of, because that was where the phone booth was Bruce had been calling from. I asked if they could get someone off the boat to call me. As soon as they heard who I was I was told, "We can't talk to you!" and they hung up.

Now this was not a good sign. I tried calling the Harbor Master but got the same response. As soon as I said what I was calling about they hung up.

Now I was getting real worried. I called United Airlines and got a seat on the next plane. At that time they flew into Hilo as well as Honolulu. The magazines had been finished so I started packing. Just before I went out the door the phone rang. It was my lawyer.

"Bob, don't fly into Hilo. They will arrest you when you land!"

"What? Why? What's going on?"

He hesitated for just a second, but long enough to make me really start to worry, and then said, "They have seized your boat and arrested the crew. My wife, the baby and I were off the boat having breakfast, and when we returned they were going to arrest us too until they heard I was a lawyer. Then they wouldn't let us go aboard, but did let us leave. We got a hotel room which is where I am calling from."

"Well, we didn't do anything wrong, so why shouldn't I just fly into Hilo?"

"Because they are waiting to arrest you!"

"For what?"

"I don't know what you have been up to," and then he hesitated, "but there were about 50 men who boarded the boat in full SWAT gear, and the crew was arrested for running guns and drugs into Hawaii."

"Look," he added, "I am going to fly to Honolulu. Meet me there. I will pick you up at the airport and we can plan on what to do."

Now, dear reader, at this point I have to tell you, we did not have any guns except the three I'd shown Customs, and we had no drugs at all, because the crew had run out of pot a little after the halfway point. This was all bullshit.

But I did as my lawyer had asked and changed my ticket from Hilo to Honolulu. As you can imagine, the flight was longer than any I had taken before. I kept going over in my alleged mind what might have caused this.

When the plane landed I was met by a pretty funny sight. My lawyer, his wife and baby, were all there waiting for me. He was in a bathing suit! I asked him why and he just said that the officials wouldn't let him board the boat to get their stuff, so they just used a credit card to fly over to Honolulu and they had checked into a hotel. I told him there was no reason I could think of this had happened. He kept saying things like, "Bob, come on, you can tell me, I'm your lawyer. What's this all about?"

Finally, I talked him into calling the Hilo police officer who had given him his card, and telling him I was here and what did they want me to do. They put him on hold a couple minutes, and then said if we flew over to Hilo we could stay on the boat that night, but we had to report to the Hilo police in the morning for me to be booked.

I still had no idea what this was all about, but we purchased tickets at the local terminal and flew back to Hilo. My lawyer just called the hotel he was at and told them to check him out. After all, they had no luggage. His wife and daughter flew back to the mainland from Honolulu.

Once we had landed in Hilo we took a cab to the boat. As I walked aboard I noticed a lot of little things were really messed up. The aft deck box was open and everything from inside it was laying all over the deck. We went below and things were all torn up. About ten minutes after we got there Bruce and the girls came on board. They had been in jail overnight and were not happy. Everyone kept asking me what I had done to cause this, and I had no earthly idea.

Some of the things that went on were actually funny. First of all, there were all kinds of people carrying guns and wearing black uniforms, bullet proof vests and carrying heavy artillery. They were from the whole alphabet of the government agencies: the FBI, Customs, ATF, DEA and local police. They had taken the girls away immediately, but kept Bruce on board asking him all kinds of questions about guns and drugs. They made him sit there for a couple hours while they played all of the VHS tapes looking for kiddy porn! They drained the engine oils to see if it was hash oil. They thought they'd hit the mother-lode when they went under my bunk and found a 10-gallon Tupperware container filled to the brim with white powder. They seemed to be extremely upset when it turned out to be flour!

They confiscated my First Aid Kit, my guns, and took about 100 photos of the cutoff I wore when I rode my Harley, which was hanging in my closet. They had pulled a couple pieces of loose teak up on deck, and pulled apart part of one of the bulkheads looking for secret compartments. They were extremely thorough. But they didn't find anything out of the ordinary. Now I was actually looking forward to talking with them in the morning.

At 9:00 a.m. we were standing in front of the Hilo Police department. We went in and asked for the sergeant that had given my lawyer his card. When we got to his office we sat down, and I asked him what this was all about. He said that they (the Hilo police) had been told that the ATF and DEA had reason to believe that we had contraband on the boat. They had contacted Customs, as Customs are not bound by the

Constitution and could board any boat in waters contiguous to open waters at any time without reasonable cause.

He said after the "raid," when nothing was found, it was all laid in his lap. I asked about my guns and First Aid kit.

"Yes, we have those," he said. And then he added, "ATF ran the serial numbers on the guns and found out they were not registered to you."

"And," he continued, "The First Aid kit contained controlled substances so it has been confiscated."

I sat there dazed for a minute.

"Now we are going to book you," he said flatly.

I asked for what, and he said possession of illegal firearms and drugs. I protested that the guns I had were registered to me, and the drugs in the First Aid kit, which turned out to be penicillin and morphine, were accompanied by a doctors prescription written for us as an ocean going vessel.

Nothing phased him and I was taken down and fingerprinted, had a mug shot taken (which is now one of my prized possessions!) and then released on OR (my own recognizance).

Now I have to tell you, this sucked. I knew the pistol was licensed to me as I had it for over a decade, and the shotgun, well, they don't register shotguns. I called a friend of mine who used to be my workout partner at the gym. Now he was the

Chief of Police in Hermosa Beach where I had my gym. I asked him if he could run my list of registered guns (I owned a few) and fax it to the police sergeant that was controlling all this.

Then we went to the Harbor Masters Office. He told me that the boat was in "constructive seizure" and we could sail between the islands but had to check in and out of each harbor as we did, and we could not leave the Hawaiian Islands.

We then found a local lawyer who didn't charge an arm and a leg and I laid out $1,500 to get everybody's arrest records expunged. They shouldn't have to pay for the rest of their life for this, like I was sure I would.

Bruce and I went back to the sergeant's office the next day to see about the guns and First Aid kit. I had paid a lot of money for that pistol, a custom AMT Hardballer with a Colt barrel, ramped and balanced. I wasn't about to let it go. My lawyer had the first flight out that a.m., and after we dropped him at the airport in a rent-a-wreck we went to the police station.

When we got up to the office he was sitting there and he had the fax from my friend Val at the Hermosa Beach Police Department. I asked if I could have the guns back now. He looked at the fax, and then at the ATF report.

"The gun that was taken off the boat was not registered to you."

"Yes it was," I replied, trying not to sound too rude. "Just check the serial number on it."

"I am," he replied. "The numbers are off."

"What do you mean off?" I asked. "I know the pistol is registered to me, I verified it with the Chief of Police in Hermosa Beach, where they were originally registered."

He looked at the papers again. "Nope!" he said. "The last three numbers are not the same."

I asked to see the papers. He handed them to me and sure enough, the numbers the ATF had turned in were, indeed, three numbers off. The last three numbers were transposed.

I said, "It's easy enough to check. Why don't you look at the gun and see what the serial number is that is on the gun?"

He grinned like he was gonna catch me now and picked up the phone.

"Bring up the .45 and shotgun we brought in from that boat, tags #..." and he rattled off some numbers.

We sat in silence a couple of minutes and the phone rang. He picked it up and listened, than said, "What do you mean it's not there? They just came in two days ago?" He hung up and turned to us.

"They can't find the shotgun right now, but they are bringing up the .45."

When it arrived he looked at the gun found the serial number and checked it against the papers. "Oh," he said. "Looks like ATF transposed the numbers."

"So I get it back now, right?"

"Yes. I guess so. I will have it released."

"How about the shotgun?" I asked.

"I'm sure they will find it. I will let you know."

"Okay, and how about the First Aid kit? I can't sail without one."

"Well, you do have some controlled substances. So we will have to hold it."

I explained to him about ocean going vessels and the letter from the doctor which was the same as a prescription.

Long story short, he had it brought up, read the letter from the doctor who had put it together, and ended up giving it back to me. I think he felt a little like the ATF, FBI and DEA had left him holding the bag.

As it turned out, there was one small item they "had on me." Lindy, the girl I was sailing with, had bought a small bag of pot from a local biker. She knew I had instigated a "no tolerance" policy on the boat so she had stashed it in the dock box. They tried to use that as a reason for the seizure, but in Hawaii, even back then, possession of less than an ounce was just a ticketing offense, so that was dropped.

The night before we sailed out to head over to Maui and try to recapture some fun on this voyage, we had dinner with the local Bike Club, the Alii. One of their members worked on the docks and told them how, the night before the raid, they had been told to stack containers in particular places so they could stage the raid without being seen. He said that they had counted at least 75 people there for the raid!

> Chapter 21 <
Voyaging in Paradise... Almost!

Once again we were cruising. With all
the police stuff behind us (or so we thought!)
we cleared out of Hilo and headed to cross the
Alenuihaha. The channel between the Big Island
and Maui was well known for big waves and
high winds so we were a little disappointed after
rounding the top of Hawaii and heading across
the channel. It was almost calm. Probably had
something to do with the Kona winds from the
week before.

As we passed into the lee of Haleakala, which
is the 10,000-foot peak on the eastern end of
Maui, we sailed close to McKena Beach, which
is at the foot of the mountain and was a beautiful
and unspoiled beach. We sailed to Lahaina, which
is the old whaling port that has turned into tourist
central, and circled the anchorage known as the
Lahaina Roads, looking for a good place to drop
our hook. Surprise! As we circled the beach I saw
a boat that looked familiar and sure enough, it was

Stone Witch! Talk about your small worlds!

We called out to Alan and then anchored as close as we could to her. Soon Alan and another crew member dinghied over to Lost Soul, and we commenced to do what cruisers do, talk story. As we talked we had a few coldies, and the afternoon was turning into a real great day.

Then we noticed a dinghy with 6 men in it, all wearing Hawaiian aloha shirts, circling our boat. We waved thinking they were tourists who had rented a dinghy, and continued our conversation. But then the dinghy pulled up along-side next to our boarding ladder. One of the men flashed a badge and soon we were, once again, boarded. They kept us up on deck while they searched down below. I had no idea what they thought they'd find since we had just had a complete rectal cavity search the week before in Hilo, but there is no arguing with men with badges and guns.

After they finished searching Lost Soul they told Alan and his crewman to go back to Stone Witch. They were going to search it as well. We sat on deck in our beanbag chairs watching as the two dinghies went to Stone Witch. In a few minutes they came up with something in their hands that was wrapped in a blanket. A while later Alan came back to Lost Soul and said they had taken his shotgun, and they found some pot in one of the crewman's bags. He had to go in the following morning to talk to them.

As it turned out they didn't arrest anyone.

Small world! SV Lost Soul an-chored next to SV Stone Witch in the Roades off of Lahaina, Maui

They gave him back the shotgun and kept the pot, telling him it was a no-no. They also told us to be sure and check out with the Harbor Master when we planned on leaving.

We hung in Lahaina for a few days and had a pretty good time playing tourist and hanging out at the Lahaina Yacht Club. The town was made for visiting sailors and tourists, and the humpback whales were playing in the channel between Maui and Lanai. At night you could hear them talking to each other when you laid in your bunk. It was great.

We bid adieu to Alan and Stone Witch after clearing out with the Harbor Master and decided to sail behind Lanai and then to a small harbor

145

we found on the charts called Lono Harbor, on the island of Molokai. It was a perfect day for sailing and we decided to haul up the spinnaker as we passed Black Manele Bay. It was a bitchin sail! We got Lost Soul up to about 8 knots, and just as we were about to come around the last bluff a 41' Coast Guard Cutter came roaring from behind the bluff at full speed and stopped in front of us, hailing us to "Drop your sails and hold your position."

Now, for those of you unfamiliar with sailing under spinnaker let me tell you, there is no fast way to drop a spinnaker. The girls tried to haul down on the spinnaker chute while Bruce eased the halyard. I stayed on the wheel trying to avoid putting a large dent in the 41' tin can that had stopped right in front of us. We got it down and then dropped the main. There were lines all over the deck, as we didn't have time to coil lines or be neat about it. Before we drifted to a halt the Coasties had launched their Zodiac and were alongside. We dropped the boarding ladder so they could come aboard.

And come aboard they did, with enough armament to stop a small Navy. They held their guns on us while three of them went below. Lindy and Marlene kept asking what this was all about. You see, Marlene, being of the single persuasion, had gone out with a couple of the Coasties when we were tied up in front of the Coast Guard Station in Radio Bay. They were the same guys that had just boarded us. But they wouldn't answer. They just stood there stone-faced.

Once again, they found nothing. As they left the boat the one that she had gone out with whispered he was sorry, but they'd been ordered to board us.

For the rest of the day we sailed in the lee of Lanai and started to enjoy the trip again. We sailed right into the entrance of Lono Harbor, where there was only one other boat, and dropped a hook and "Med Moored" to the concrete quay. Lono Harbor had been built a while ago, but never used. The breakwater was high and sound, so the anchorage was calm. But the concrete quay had started to crumble a little, and there was absolutely nothing on the shore. Just dirt, a couple trees, and a dirt road that led up the hill to God knows where.

That night we built a fire ashore and roasted some hot dogs we had aboard. It was a beautiful night. We hung out for the whole next day, and then decided to head for Oahu where we would stay for the next couple weeks, as I would have to fly back and work on the magazine.

The sail to Oahu was pretty brisk. The winds had come up to regular trade-winds velocity, about 25-30 knots ashore and 35-40 knots in the channels. As shore was not an option, we opted for the channel, with a reefed main and headsail. (Oh, yeah, I forgot to mention while in Hilo we had fixed the broken spreader and rear window!)

I was checking out the chart of Oahu and saw this beautiful little bay that looked like it would be the perfect anchorage after we crossed the channel between Molokai and Oahu. It was called Hanauma Bay. Okay, those of you who know Hawaii will now be chuckling to yourselves, or out loud. Those of you who may not be familiar, let me fill you in on the joke.

You see, Hanauma Bay is a world class diving destination, and it is a Nature Preserve. BUT, it doesn't say that on my chart! So I see this perfect little bay and decided that's for us!

As I had learned, you don't want to arrive at a strange harbor in the dark, so I had left in time for us to arrive just before sunset. As we approached it was absolutely beautiful! A hundred shades of blue water ending at a white sand beach with palm trees. A true Polynesian paradise! So we looked for a good sand bottom and dropped our hook in about 50 feet of water. I couldn't believe that there were no boats anchored there!

Just as the sun set we donned our snorkels and masks and did a quick dive. It was unbelievable! That night we slept like babes in our mothers' arms. No swell, no noise, and a perfect anchorage.

And it was also illegal for us to be there.

This we found out the first thing in the morning when a rowboat came out and told us, in no uncertain terms, that anchoring here was a total no-no. We invited them aboard and after a few minutes one of them said that we really looked "cool" anchored there, and he said he would ask the manager if we could stay for a day since we had anchored in sand and not near coral.

They said yes! How kewl was that? All day long people swam out and around our boat. It was a perfect day as we swam, snorkeled and even managed to wipe the bottom down with green pads to get her clean.

The next morning people waved to us from the beach as we carefully raised the anchor and headed out of the bay. Once again, it was a great sail, as we ran downwind along the shore of Oahu and headed towards the Ala Wai Yacht Harbor. Sailing past Diamond Head made us feel like we were truly in Hawaii!

Entering the Ala Wai can be a daunting task the first time. The entrance is about 100 feet wide and there are surfers riding waves right next to you! The entrance is dredged, but knowing that doesn't help when the water is so clear it looks like you are on the bottom, and swells start to raise you up as you enter.

Once inside we stopped at the fuel dock, and I went to the Harbor Master to "check in" and see about a slip for a couple weeks. They had one available and soon we were tied snug as a bug in a rug, and ready to enjoy a day or two in Honolulu before I had to fly out to go to work.

> Chapter 22 <
Is there no end to this?

I had been back in the office about three days when I got a frantic call from Lindy. She was close to tears.

"They boarded us again. This time they took the First Aid kit and your gun again."

I could tell she was really upset. But she wasn't anywhere near as upset as I was getting. I called my lawyer, and he made a couple calls.

"You need to talk to the head of Customs for this to end," he said. Then he gave me a number for Customs in Hawaii. I made the call. Soon I was talking with the head of the Customs office in Honolulu. He said I should come in and "discuss" it. I agreed and got a red-eye for Hawaii late that night.

Bruce picked me up at the airport in a rent-a-car and we drove directly to his office. We got there about a half hour before he got in, so we had a cup of coffee across the street and tried to figure out what this was all about. We couldn't!

When he arrived we were brought into his office. In a nutshell he told me they knew that I was running guns and drugs into Hawaii, and that they knew I was working with the Hells Angels doing it.

I was flabbergasted! I asked him what gave him that idea and all he said was they knew what was going on, so I should just fess up. He then went on to tell me that they knew I was an associate of the Hells Angels because they had video of me at the acting President's house a year or so earlier, and they knew that I had visited Sonny Barger when he was in Folsom Prison.

He then went on to tell me that they had an undercover agent at a meeting between the two local outlaw motorcycle clubs, and overheard that I was sailing over and had guns and good drugs. To top it all off one of the members of the Hells Angels died in a plane crash on his way to Hawaii on the day I arrived, and Sonny flew in to pick up the body while we were in Hilo.

Somehow they put all this together to make me guilty of running guns and drugs.

I sat in stunned silence as he told me how they "knew" I was guilty, and how they were going to get proof soon. After he finished I sat there quiet and tried to organize my thoughts, as I was pretty flustered by all this.

"Okay, I see why you think I might be guilty of something. I guess the question I have is, IF I am not guilty of any of this, how could I prove it to you?"

He sat for a minute and thought it over. "How do you explain what has been going on?" he asked.

I then explained most of the stuff away. I had interviewed Sonny Barger for an article in a number of magazines including Biker and Easyriders as well as a the Beach Peoples' Easy Reader Newspaper, and that was why I had visited him in Folsom. I had gone to talk with the Cisco, a member of the HA after the interview, and as I was leaving he laughed and said, 'Smile for the cameras," pointing at an open window across the street. That had put me on a list somewhere.

As for the two clubs, as it turned out one of the clubs was the na Kua'Ana Motorcycle Club, who's President, Francis Diaz, owned a custom motorcycle shop and I had been there a couple times shooting some of the bikes he built for features in my motorcycle magazines. The President of the Devils Breed Motorcycle Club, who was also at the meeting, was none other than Rat, who had lived on my boat a couple years earlier in California.

The only thing I could think of was, I did have a small collection of unusual guns and I did have some extremely good drugs back then, but not on the boat, and I had quit doing drugs.

He thought about this for a minute or two. "Okay," he said. Go to the ATF offices here in Honolulu and get a cruising permit for your gun, and then get a permit for your First Aid kit from the DEA or FDA saying it should contain controlled substances, and we will see what we can do."

Bruce and I walked out of Customs and went looking for ATF and the FDA. As it turned out, they were both in the same building, just a couple blocks away.

First we went into the ATF offices. I approached a guy sitting at one of the desks and told him my story. Before I had finished half the office was standing around listening and laughing. I didn't see the humor, until I finished.

"There is no such thing as a cruising permit for a gun," he said.

I looked at Bruce, and he looked at me. "Er, can you call this guy and tell him that?" I asked, handing him the man's card.

"Sure," he said. "No problem."

He had a short conversation on the phone and ended it with something like, "...and there is no cruising permit for a gun." He then told me the man understood and it wouldn't be a problem.

So now it was off to the FDA. This was even funnier, as they had no idea what a cruising permit for a First Aid kit would be. Once again, I handed him the card, and he called the man at Customs. He let him know that it was standard procedure for cruising boats to have a letter from a doctor with a cruising kit that contained penicillin and morphine in case of major accident while at sea.

"He said you should come on back to Customs," the man said when he got off the phone.

We walked back to the Customs building and were ushered into the office.

"Okay, we are going to give you your gun and First Aid kit back, but we are going to be watching you. Your boat is still under constructive seizure."

"How do I take care of that? I asked. "Nothing was found, and I am not guilty of anything."

"Well, there was still the half-ounce of marijuana that was found in the dock box" He said.

"Okay, let's talk about that. It wasn't on my boat. I never had possession of it, so even if it was mine, which it wasn't," I agreed with him, "isn't that a misdemeanor? It's not a reason to seize my boat, is it?"

He thought for a second or two.

"Okay, I can have the seizure lifted, but you are going to have to pay a release of seizer fee." He said.

"Say what?" I asked. "Nothing was found, why do I have to pay a fine?"

"Oh," he quickly said, "It's not a fine. It's a fee."

As I wrote the check out, I was just glad to get it all behind me. This wasn't cruising, and it wasn't fun. I just wanted it over.

Just as a little side note here: For the next 5 years every time I entered the U.S. I would get sent over to the "Group W" bench, where I would get a rectal exam and a thorough search. I finally had to have my lawyer threaten a lawsuit for harassment after 15 times without ever having anything found.

> Chapter 23 <
Cruising at Last in Hawaii

Now we were free of any restrictions. We sailed down to Kauai and anchored in Nawiliwili Harbor. It was a well protected anchorage with a nice stream that emptied into it. There was a small marina there, but it was too small and too shallow for Lost Soul, so we stayed outside the marina but inside the protected anchorage.

We rented a car and drove around the island, visiting the "Hawaiian Grand Canyon" on the south and the Pali Coast on the north side. We played tourist and even loaded our dinghy onto the rent-a-car and drove it to the mouth of the Wailua River, then motored all the way up to the Fern Grotto near the start. It was a beautiful trip.

We were actually starting to have a good time once the boardings stopped. We sailed around the island to Hanalei Bay and took the dinghy up it as far as we could go. Then we took Lost Soul out and sailed past the Na Pali Coast, which is beautiful. It rains there more than anywhere else on Earth, so we opted to head back to the sunny part of Hawaii.

Sailing back to Oahu from Kauai taught us a lesson about sailing in Hawaii. The winds always run from the Big Island to Kauai. In order to get back to the Big Island you have to beat into some hellatious seas and winds. But we were cruisers and we wanted to cruise the islands. After another quick trip (by air!) back to the mainland to put an issue to bed, we started our sail back to the Big Island to see the Kona Coast.

The first day it was a hard beat to weather right into 30-knot winds and 12- to 15-foot seas, and we made it as far as Lono Harbor. Over the years this would become our regular hangout

Bob at the helm of the catamaran Sea Smoke off of Waikaloa on the Big Island of Hawaii

whenever we sailed Hawaii. We stayed for a day and then sailed in behind Lanai, in the lee of these great cliffs there, and spent the night anchored off the Pinnacles which is a great dive spot.

In the morning we sailed to McKena Beach and spent the afternoon enjoying the white sand and blue waters. Back then it was virtually unknown to tourists, and it was the perfect Hawaiian beach.

Then came the tough part. Crossing the Alenuihaha. The 13,000+ foot mountains on the Big Island and the 10,000 foot Haleakala cause a venturi effect that brings on the trades and multiplies them. We made as much northing as we could, and then tried to let the boat fall off a little as we crossed. It was blustery and a real adventure, but soon we were sailing into Kealakekua Bay. This is where Captain Cook first anchored when he "discovered" Hawaii. (Like the Hawaiians didn't know it was there?)

We pulled in around the hooked point and anchored against the cliff. Today it is illegal to anchor there because of the coral, but when we were there we could do like we did in Cabo, drop 150 feet of chain with the hook down, and then back until we almost hit the cliffs. Then we would tie off to a notch on the cliffs and be settled in.

After spending a day there, we sailed north to Kailua-Kona. This is a great little town on a beautiful bay, and it's a decent anchorage except during a south wind. They call those Kona Storms, and having experienced one, we didn't want to experience another.

We settled in and were enjoying our sightseeing. One day, when I was sitting on the sea wall in front of the Banyon Tree Court, just in front of Hilo Hattie's retail store, I heard a "tap, tap, tap," and looked around. A man was putting up a For Rent sign on a small open storefront. I got up and wandered over.

"How much is it renting for?" I asked.

I never should have asked. A day later I was signing a rental agreement on a location where we were going to open "The Pirates Den" and sell cigarettes, cigars, paraphernalia for smoking, and rent bikes. Lindy loved the place and said she would stay there and run it. My partner back at Hermosa High came in on it with me, and he shipped a bunch of stuff from our store in Hermosa Beach. In less than a week we were store owners in Kailua-Kona.

During the setup, and just to make us not feel too secure here, a Kona Storm did start to come in. The boat started rocking and we hauled the anchor, heading around the point to where they said a small marina was located. It was called Honokohau. And it was small. Very small.

The entrance was dredged from the reef and it had a dog-leg entrance. The problem with this was I couldn't see into the harbor. I had to commit and go in before seeing how big the slips were and how deep it was, and they were not answering the VHF.

The slips (at that time) were very small, all under 40' feet, and the depth was iffy at best. I made the dog-leg turns, and as I entered the harbor I realized that there was no place for me to go and that it got shallow ahead. I had no choice. I dropped the hook. I think we were in, like 10 feet of water. Lost Soul drew 7 feet. I let out about 50 feet of chain and backed to set it. I couldn't go much further or I'd be in the entrance of the harbor.

We dropped the stern hook into the dinghy and Bruce took it back to the entrance and dropped it. We tightened it up and there we sat, in the middle of the little harbor, with people looking at us like we were nuts. But boats could get around us and the wind was building, so I didn't have much of a choice.

The storm only lasted about two days. When it was over I slowly backed out of the harbor. This is more difficult than it sounds, as Lost Soul was a Taiwan Turkey, and in reverse it steered about the same as a car with four flat tires.

We spent about another week in Kona, and then went back to Oahu where I started to get ready for the sail back to the mainland. Lindy and Marlene were staying in Kona and we'd rented a small condo so I could come back and do some SCUBA diving. That was one of the reasons Daniel, my partner in the head shop, wanted to open the store, so we could get certified and do some diving.

> Chapter 24 <
Once More into the Breach.
Where Only the Dumb Dare Go!

It felt good to cast off the dock lines leaving the Ala Wai Harbor in Waikiki. There was too much civilization there, and I needed to go out and get some sea time to relax my jangled nerves after all the legal hassles we had while cruising Hawaii.

There is a relaxed calm that comes over me when I set sail on a major voyage. I think it has to do with the fact that once I am "out there" I am responsible for my own actions, and if I have planned well, everything should be fine.

Leaving Hawaii the sailing directions said to head north to about 40° and then turn east to come into landfall somewhere between San Francisco and Vancouver. That's what it said, so that was what we planned. It would be two or three more trips from Hawaii before I realized that the sailing directions were written for square-rigged boats that sailed downwind well. When Lost Soul sailed downwind she didn't handle well. In fact, she wallowed like an overfed pig!

But that was what they said, so that was what we did.

For this trip we had an all-male crew. Well, three were male and one wasn't so sure. More on that in a bit.

Here's what happened. Since we were leaving Lindy and Marlene in Hawaii to run the new store, we had to get other crew. When we got back to the Ala Wai we posted a notice looking for crew for the sail to the mainland. I didn't want to do it with just Bruce and me, as that would mean long watches which I would prefer not to have.

A couple days after we posted the notice one of our neighbors came over. He lived on a boat there and planned to make the trip in a few months, so he wanted to see what it would be like. He was an experienced sailor and seemed to know boats pretty well, so now we were three.

I could see us doing it with three people. That would mean 3 hours on and 6 off. Not too bad. We stocked the boat and set the date to leave.

The day before we were to leave a guy showed up at the dock and asked if we needed more crew. A quick calculation (2 hour watches, that's a good thing) and I asked him to come on board. He asked where we were going to land, and I said probably San Francisco. He said that was perfect, as that's where he wanted to go. He said he could cook, and the deal was sealed.

We still had our rental car, so I asked Bruce

to drive him to get his stuff, and figured we'd take off at sunset so we could spend the night at sea going around Oahu and enjoying our last night in the islands. I finished packing away the stores and as soon as they returned I took the rental car up to Budget to drop it off, and walked back to the boat. I was anxious to get underway.

Just before sunset we dropped the dock lines for the last time in the foreseeable future, and motored out of the Ala Wai. The surfers were still riding the waves alongside the entrance channel as we hoisted the mainsail. I brought up the mizzen as Bruce popped the headsail, and we were California bound. It was here I got the first inkling that perhaps I had made a mistake bringing along the newcomer.

"So what time do you think we'll get into San Francisco?" he asked.

I looked at him, assuming he was joking. "About two or three weeks," I responded. "Probably around 8:00 a.m.," I added, jokingly.

He stared at me for a couple seconds.

"No, really," he went on, "What time?"

I was starting to think he was serious.

"Well, it's about 2,300 miles and we average a little over 100 miles a day, so we are probably looking at about 18-25 days."

"That can't be," he said with assurance. "I just flew in from San Francisco yesterday and it only took 3-4 hours. How could it take so long?" He was, indeed, serious.

We talked for awhile and I got the whole story. It seems that his boyfriend had given him a one-way ticket to Hawaii for his birthday. He didn't tell him it was one way, of course. He didn't find out until the plane landed in Hawaii. It was the first time he'd ever flown, and he was very excited. When the plane landed he stayed in his seat for the return flight. Soon the flight attendant came and told him he'd have to get off the plane. He asked if he couldn't just stay until it turned around. It was then he found out it was a one-way ticket.

And he only had a few dollars on him.

He asked a policeman in the airport what he should do, and it was suggested that he go to the YMCA where he could get a bed for the night and sleep. Then the policeman suggested he go to the marina. He said a lot of boats were looking for crew to go back to the mainland, and maybe he could get a ride.

And so he did. And so he was sitting here on the Lost Soul as we were saying aloha to the Hawaiian Islands.

As night set in we watched the lights go dim behind us, and by the next day we were out of sight of land. We were sailing again. I gathered the crew on the aft deck for the reading of the rules. I guess if we were to have a Rule #5 it would be to let everyone know what the rules aboard are.

First we covered the watch schedule, and I drilled into their heads how important it was to stay awake on watch. I explained that when they were on watch and the other crew members were asleep, their lives were in their hands.

I also explained about water rationing. This was before we could afford a watermaker, and we only carried 125 gallons of water. I explained that we would wash dishes in saltwater, which we had run to the sink, and only do the final rinse in fresh.

Same with showers. We would wash with saltwater, either by bucket over the side, or if we were becalmed we might stop to wash up and take a swim, but fresh water was only to be used for rinsing your hair, and not more than three times a week.

Of course, I had to show the newbies how the head worked and where things were stored. Then we went thru the safety drill. If we had to go overboard I showed them where the ditch bag was, gave everyone a job to do, from grabbing as much food as they could carry to cutting loose the inflatable dinghy (our life raft!) which hung from the aft davits. We kept a sharp knife in a sheath laced to the aft shroud for just such a purpose.

We discussed a cooking schedule and everyone agreed to rotate the cooking duties. Whoever was going to have the next cooking duty would do the dishes. It looked like everything was going to be okay.

Our first new crewman, Mark, who had his own boat in the marina, was about as good a crew as you could want. But Eugene was another story.

He was not the brightest light bulb in the box. He finally started to understand that it would, indeed, take two-three weeks to get back to San Francisco, but he could not seem to grasp the fact that a sailboat used the wind to move. When we shut off the engine he almost freaked out.

"How are we going to get home if we turn off the engine?" he asked.

It took me awhile, but I was finally able to convince him that we actually moved faster under sail than we did under motor. And besides, we didn't have enough fuel to motor all the way. At this he really freaked out. We carried 100 gallons of fuel. We burned 1.25 gallons an hour if we were becalmed, making about 6.5 knots. So our motoring distance was limited to about 525 miles total, and it was about 2,300 miles to San Francisco.

After a few days Eugene started to settle into the lifestyle. One evening I was sitting on watch and Eugene came up on deck. Bruce and Mark were sleeping below.

"I really like Bruce, but I don't think he likes me," he said.

This was understandable, as Bruce was a bodybuilder who used to run my gym, and he was in very good shape. He was also extremely heterosexual. I tried to explain this to Eugene, but he kept talking about how he was going to make him like him before the cruise was over. No matter how hard I tried, I couldn't convince him it was a futile effort.

About 7-8 days out I was sleeping in my bunk in the aft cabin and woke up to heed the call of nature. From my bunk I could look up thru the aft hatch and see whoever was on watch. I could see Eugene sitting there and he looked as if he were asleep. I went thru the cabin to the companionway and looked up. Sure enough, he was sitting with his head on a cushion, with the autopilot on, sleeping like a baby.

I went up the companionway ladder and stood in front of him. "Eugene!!" I yelled. "What the hell are you doing sleeping while on watch?"

He jumped up and his eyes were wide open now. As he had no answer, he just stood there not knowing what to do. I sat down opposite him and explained to him how important it was to stay awake. If a ship were to come over the horizon it could be on us in just a few minutes, and everyone on board depended on each other to keep awake on watch.

He apologized over and over, saying it would never happen again.

The next day Bruce was telling me that he was getting really annoyed with Eugene, as he kept hitting on him. Bruce didn't take well to this and told me if he kept it up he was going to smack him. I asked him to try and be patient. Just a week or so and we should be nearing land.

When we got up into the high 30° area we started to make some easting. It was turning cool, and the worst thing was I couldn't get a noon site for 3-4 days at a time. We had to go by dead reckoning.

One morning I awoke and found that we were surrounded by a sea of Man O' War jelly fish. Not just hundreds. Not thousands even, but millions of them, and none larger than about 2 inches across. As far as the eye could see we had jellyfish. We sailed thru them for almost two days and nights. Then one morning, just as fast as they had came on us, they were behind us. It had been a real battle because we couldn't run the salt water pumps without picking the little suckers up in the intakes, and getting them out was a real bitch!

When we got up to the 40° line we were finally headed eastward toward land. The water up there was really cold. As I recall, we joked about it being 40° water at 40° latitude. This wouldn't have been too much of a problem if we hadn't hit that stupid fishing net!

Yup! We were sailing along at about 4 knots when all of a sudden we came to a stop. As there was no land around we checked behind us to see if we were dragging anything. We were. We were dragging about 40 feet of fishing net trailing behind us, and it slowed us to a standstill.

Now, this was only my second major crossing and I had not made all the proper emergency preparations. I learned this when I realized that we did not have a wetsuit on board. And why, you may be asking yourself, would one need a wetsuit? For just such an occasion as this. A big fishing net wrapped on our prop, the wind dying, and we can't run the motor.

Someone was going to have to go into the 40° water and cut us loose.

Bruce was the first to volunteer. He put on a swimming suit (it was about 55° outside and pretty cold) and I handed him the large knife that we would use to cut the dinghy loose in an emergency, and he went down the ladder.

Now, I don't know if this is a medical fact, but I can tell you this... When he got into the water and swam back to the rudder area he said it was cold, but it was so cold that every time he tried to put his head underwater he couldn't do it.

Bruce learning that you never volunteer!

169

His diaphragm would contract and he had to keep his head above the water. Quickly I got the knife from him and tied it to the end of the boat hook. Try though he may, and he gave it a valiant effort indeed, he could not cut the net loose.

He had a hard time climbing the ladder. If he had stayed in the water over 15 minutes hypothermia could have killed him. As it was, the 10 or so minutes that he spent in the water took its toll on his muscles, and he could barely climb out.

For the next few hours I fumed at my stupidity. No wetsuit. We had a net keeping us from motoring and the wind had all but died. It was cold, and I can tell you that I was not a happy skipper!

As my wife can attest to, I don't give up easily. I tried everything I could think of. We dropped the dinghy into the water and tried to cut the net loose from inside the dinghy. We did manage to cut the part that was trailing behind us, but not enough to free the prop.

I finally just bit the bullet, so to speak, and decided I would have to get that net off the prop or we could sit out there forever. I went below and wiped Vaseline all over my body. Then I put on a sweatshirt and sweat pants, and wiped more Vaseline over the surface of them. I then put on a pair of Levis and another pullover shirt, and put Vaseline all over them.

I walked up on deck looking like the Pillsbury Doughboy.

Going down the ladder I gritted my teeth and said there was no way I was going to come back on board unless the prop was free. They handed me the boat hook and I went in. I can tell you with complete honesty that all of the clothes and Vaseline did absolutely nothing! As I hit the water it was like ice cubes all over my body.

I got in and went back by the rudder. I had a line tied to me from on deck just in case I couldn't get out later. I was going to get this boat clear if it killed me.

And it almost did!

When I tried to put my head under the water my diaphragm would contract and I would suck sea water into my mouth. I just could not put my head under without taking in copious amounts of ice-cold sea water. I hacked and jabbed at the net, and nothing seemed to be happening. Finally I hooked the net with the boat hook and just jerked it with all my might. Some of the line that made up the net broke!

I hooked it again, and again I was able to jerk it hard enough to break some of the lines. But I also noticed that I was starting to feel very warm and thought, because I was getting used to the water, maybe I could stay in and finish the job.

And then I remembered a very cold May evening in the highest part of New Mexico when I was riding my Harley and didn't have a jacket. I had gotten hypothermia, and soon I felt warm all over. I was about to pull over to get some rest when a Highway Patrolman pulled me over for felonious existing (that's a crime when you are an outlaw biker!). When he saw my face he had me get into his car, and I started shaking like a paint mixer at Home Depot.

There was no doubt about it, I was getting hypothermia. I made my way back to the ladder and tried to move my feet up and onto a rung. I couldn't do it. I couldn't move my legs.

The guys started to pull on the rope that was tied around my waist and I got high enough to get a foot on the ladder. Slowly I made it up on deck. I got out of my clothes as fast as I could and wrapped myself in a large blanket. Then I started to shiver, right down to my bones.

In the meantime Bruce took the boat hook and was able to hook it into the net. He jerked on it and it kept tearing. He worked on it for about half an hour, and by then I had warmed up. I worked on it for a little while longer and all of a sudden, viola! It came free!

We were free!

I started the motor and dropped it into gear. The boat pulled away from the net and we watched it disappear behind us.

Life was good again!

> Chapter 25 <
Murder? No. Too Much Paperwork!

The "romance" between Eugene and Bruce was getting comical. Bruce did everything he could to avoid contact with Eugene, but we were on a 51-foot "island" and there were not a lot of places to escape to.

One evening after we had dinner I was walking up the companionway ladder, which was right next to the galley, and Eugene was washing the dishes. But something was wrong. He was filling the sink with fresh water. That was a no-no as we had very limited water and had covered that in the original briefing.

I asked him what he was doing, and he just said, "Washing the dishes."

I got off the ladder and walked over, shutting off the fresh water.

"Don't you remember when I told you the dishes had to be washed using the saltwater foot pump?" I asked rather gruffly.

"Yeah, but this is a lot easier. I don't know

why we have to do it in saltwater."

"Because we will run out of fresh water if we use it all washing dishes!" I exclaimed.

He thought about that for a minute and then came back with, "But we can just fill up with fresh water when we get into San Francisco." That was his answer.

I shook my head and told him, in no uncertain terms, from now on saltwater only to wash the dishes. As I walked away I could see him shaking his head as if he thought I was nuts.

A couple nights later I woke up for a nature call and once again it looked like Eugene was asleep at the wheel. Once again I went thru the cabin and up the companionway, and once again he was, indeed, sleeping. This time I grabbed the front of his shirt and jerked him off the bench until his face was about 3 inches from my face.

"You do not sleep on watch!!" I yelled into his face. His eyes were wide open and he was obviously shaken. That was what I wanted to do, because my life was also in his hands when he's on watch. I am also pretty sure I had a great case of "dragon breath," having woken up after we had a meal of beans and hot dogs.

I sat down next to him and tried to calm down. "Listen," I said to him, "sailing can be a dangerous proposition. If a ship were to be coming at us, we are so small that they probably wouldn't even see us. Big ships move at 20-25 knots, and the horizon is only about 13 miles distant. That

174

means if one were coming at us from the front,
with us doing 5 knots and them doing 25 knots,
they could collide with us in a matter of minutes.
You HAVE to stay awake and alert on watch."

Then I closed with, "Do you understand?"

He nodded yes and we sat there in silence for
awhile. Then he said, out of nowhere, "You know
Bruce is really hurting my feelings. He thinks
because he's a big guy that I am afraid of him, but
I'm not."

This came out of left field. But he was right.
Bruce was very muscled and in great shape.
Eugene was about 5'6" and had to weigh in at
about 125 pounds.

He continued, "I could kill him while he
sleeps." He said it as if he was talking about the
weather.

"What the hell are you talking about?" I
asked, incredulous that he would say something
like that.

"I could even poison him when I cook
dinner," he continued to muse, as if I wasn't even
sitting there.

"Look dude," I said. "You better straighten
yourself out here. We only have a few more days
at sea, and then you'll be back in San Francisco.
Won't your boyfriend be waiting for you?" I
asked, remembering his story about the one-way
ticket to Hawaii.

"No, I only knew him a few days, and he just
wanted to have a place to stay. I'll bet that's why

he gave me the one-way ticket." He mused.

I told him to get his shit together and went back down, shaking my head. Why had I not vetted him better? I knew better than to take a stranger on as crew, but I had overlooked that rule.

So I guess we be looking at Rule #6. Be sure to know who you take with you as crew!

This was really brought to the forefront a couple days later. I had gotten a noon site and figured we were pretty close to spotting the Farallon Islands. The Farallon's sit about 30 miles out from the Golden Gate Bridge and landfall. I figured we were probably looking at our last night out. I also figured we should be getting some ship traffic soon, as we had seen 3-4 big boats that day. I told everyone to keep a sharp lookout and turned in just after dinner. I wanted to be up early and try to be the one who gets to shout "Land Ho!"

Once again, that night I awoke for my nature call and once again, believe it or not, Eugene was sound asleep on watch. Now I was pissed. I knew there had to be a lot of traffic, and this was really a dangerous place to be in a small sailboat.

I grabbed my .45 AMT Hardballer and cocked it. I walked thru the boat and up the companionway. He was sound asleep. At first I seriously considered dong something I knew I would regret later, but common sense took hold of me. I stood there for a minute with the gun cocked and in my hand. Then I put it about a foot away from his ear, aimed out to sea, and pulled the trigger.

It was loud!

It was very loud!

Eugene jumped up and peed all over himself.

"I told you you cannot sleep on watch!! What do we have to do to get that thru your thick skull??!!" I asked, rather loudly.

Bruce and Mark came running up the companionway. "What's up! What's happening?"

I stood there with the gun in my hand and Eugene sat there in his piss-filled seat holding his hand over his ear.

"Did you shoot him?" Bruce asked, and I could swear I saw a smile on his lips.

"No. I just caught him sleeping for the third time. Take a look around you? Look at all the ship traffic!"

Then I looked at Eugene. The look in his eyes was far scarier than anything I had seen in awhile. He was looking at Bruce and saw the smile when he asked me if I shot him. His look was murderous.

"Bruce," I said quietly. "Go down below and get those large wire ties we have in the workroom.

We had brought a couple of foot-long wire ties as spares for the ones that held our Aqua-Lift water separator in place in the engine room.

When he came up we took Eugene forward to the mainmast area.

"We are going to keep him here until we get into shore," I told the three of them. With that we tied his arms around the mast after settling him into one of the beanbags we keep on deck for comfort.

It was just before dawn and the Farallon Islands were in sight. I figured we would be pulling into a dock in about 6 hours, and this guy was clearly unhinged.

I went and checked the tide charts. We were in luck, we should be hitting the Golden Gate Bridge just after low tide, so we would have a fairly easy entrance to San Francisco.

We had filed a float-plan in Hawaii before leaving, so I radioed the Coast Guard as we passed the Farallons and let them know we were arriving from Hawaii. They told us thanks, and since we'd sailed from a U.S. port to a U.S. port, we wouldn't have to clear in.

We got into a dock near the Golden Gate Yacht Club about two miles inside the bay and tied up. I asked Mark to go cut Eugene loose and to help him gather his stuff and get off the boat. It only took a couple minutes and he was gone.

And good riddance!

Oh, yeah, but one thing was missing after he'd gone. He had stolen Bruce's jacket as he passed his bunk. Bruce didn't mind. He was just glad to have him out of his hair. We never heard from him again!

> Chapter 26 <
A Few More Trips and an Offer I Couldn't Refuse!

Over the next couple years I sailed Lost Soul all over the Pacific. I made three or four trips to Mexico, sailing south as far as Zihuatanejo and Acapulco. I also made a couple more trips to Hawaii, but none were as interesting as the very first crossing.

As time passed I added a lot of creature comforts to the boat, eventually adding Loran (once it became affordable!). But I always kept her in as prime a condition as I could. I varnished her brightwork at least every three months and she looked beautiful.

Yeah, okay, I was obsessive about that, but my pride was vindicated one afternoon when I was at my mooring in King Harbor Marina. By then I'd owned the boat about 7 years. One afternoon Worm and I were sunning ourselves on deck when a man in a dinghy started to circle my boat. I waved, he waved, and then he came over to the boarding ladder.

"You interested in selling the boat?" he asked bluntly.

As I am sure you know, boats always seem to have a price. At the time I still owed about $90,000 on the boat. So we started talking.

As it turned out, the boat he used to own was the one I'd fallen in love with years before, the Jade Lady. She was a Formosa 41. As I've said, I do have an affinity for Formosa boats! This one was known as the Sea Wolf 41 - traditional - with a bowsprit and wineglass stern. And, she was detailed to perfection! I had actually looked at her because I thought she was the most beautiful boat I had ever seen in King Harbor. Her hull was dark green with gold stripping, and her teak always shined. In fact, what I had done to Lost Soul was due quite a bit to Jade Lady. And it was this guy, his name was Rich Hall, who had created Jade Lady. No wonder he liked Lost Soul!

It seems awhile back he got an offer he couldn't refuse and sold the boat. He'd moved up to a little place in Northern California named Oroville where he bought 40 acres, subdivided it into 5-acre parcels and built a custom house on one of the lots to try and make his fortune.

As we all know, sometimes the best-laid plans of mice and men go awry. Just after he'd finished building the first house there was a fire at the telephone pole processing area a few miles away. Fighting that fire had fouled the water table beneath homes in that area. It would be years before the well water would be good.

When he came down to King Harbor to visit friends he'd seen Lost Soul sitting at her mooring. She looked so much like the Jade Lady as far as finish and style that he just had to take a look at her.

To make a long story short, when I asked him what he was thinking about when it came to a price, he hesitated. It seems he was land-poor. He had the acreage and house in Oroville, and another building lot outside Palm Springs, but little to no cash. What he did offer me was the property in Oroville and Palm Springs, and to take over the payments. A quick calculation in my feeble little head said I had to listen to the offer. I only had about $20,000 into the boat after all this time (aside what I had spent on maintenance and things, but I always mark that down to living expenses).

A few days later Rich, an old friend of mine named Danny Sprouse, and I were on a plane headed to Sacramento. Danny Sprouse was one of my best friends and had managed a few car dealerships in his past. He was one of the best negotiators I knew, so I asked him to come along and help me with this deal.

When we landed in Sacramento I rented a Lincoln Town Car (Hey! They didn't cost much to rent and were really comfortable!) and we were soon headed north to Oroville. Danny did most of the talking as we drove, telling Rich how great the boat was, and how bad it was for him that the land was in Oroville and the water table was fouled. He'd done a few comparisons and found out about the Kopper's Fire, when the water was all polluted in 1984. That had been a year or two earlier, and they estimated it could be 10 years before the well water would be usable.

We drove to the house and it was a nice 3-bedroom custom-built home. He had planned on selling it for $200,000, but with the bad well no one would buy it.

As we drove back to Sacramento, Danny worked on Rich, and soon we had come to a deal. He would turn over the house and 40 acres, as well as the building lot in Palm Springs, and take over the payments on Lost Soul.

Bob & Brother Al

It took a few months, but we soon moved the 35 acres that were still undeveloped and came out very well. The building lot in Palm Springs brought in a little more than expected, and soon I found myself with enough funds to buy another boat!

And this time for CASH!

> Chapter 27 <
Finding Predator

As I have said, I truly love the Formosa built Bill Garden designs. So I started looking. I found one I really liked down in San Diego, but the owner wanted about $180k and I didn't want to pay that much, so I kept looking.

Then I found one at Pier 39 in San Francisco. This was before the sea lions had completely taken over the marina there, and only the first three docks were infested with them.

It was a Formosa 51 and the price, at $125k, was fair enough. The owner allowed me to stay on it for the night and I was close to buying it. But something bothered me about it. I don't know what it was, but I was not comfortable on the boat.

In the morning I returned the keys to him and begged off. I didn't know why, but it just "didn't feel right."

So maybe we have Rule #8. On the right boat you will feel comfortable on it from the start.

In the years since, when I would give a

seminar and people would ask what to look for when buying a boat, my only advice would be, "If it feels right, it's the right boat."

So I was driving the long drive down Highway 1 back towards Redondo Beach. I had just gotten a cell phone and it rang as I drove thru Ventura. It seems that the boat I had looked at that was too expensive had just had a price reduction. He'd dropped the price to $110,000. I told the broker I was already on the road and would see her in a few hours.

Two and a half hours later I arrived at the home of the owner of the Formosa 51, in the Coronado Cays. Behind his house was a private dock. On one side sat a Swan, obviously set up for racing, and opposite it sat a very nice Formosa 51. I honestly don't even remember the name of the boat, but as the broker met me in front of the house she said the owner was out back arguing with someone who had flown in from Hawaii to see the boat, and was making him an offer.

We walked back and sure enough, standing on the lawn were two men, nose to nose in negotiating. As I approached the boat it looked great. Clean and well maintained. I boarded her and walked into the companionway. It was the aft steering station version. Below decks the boat looked like new. When I got to the bottom of the steps I opened the salon floor and the engine looked like it was brand new. I turned to the broker.

"Go tell the man I will take it," I said, reaching into my pocket.

I had the $10,000 on me that I was going to give to the man in San Francisco as a down payment.

"How much do you want to offer?" She asked.

"He's asking $110,000 right? That's what I am offering. Get out there before he sells it to that guy."

I wandered through the boat and everywhere I looked the boat looked like new. It was a 1981, so it was 7 years old, but obviously it had been well taken care of. It only had 350 hours on the motor.

A couple minutes later the broker came down with the owner. He was smiling.

"I want you to know," he said with a grin, "how much I appreciate your timing. That guy had come in from Hawaii and was offering me $90,000. I kept telling him no, but he has been arguing with me for almost an hour. It felt so good when you bought the boat so I could just smile at him and say, 'Have a nice day'!"

We made arrangements to haul the boat in a couple days and I headed back to Redondo Beach. I knew it was the right boat.

It was kinda funny when it came time to take the boat to the haul-out for the survey. Bruce had come down with me and it was the two of us and the broker who backed the boat out of the slip and headed out to the narrow channel to get out of the

Coronado Cays. We were about halfway up the channel, which was dredged to 10 feet, when the boat's motor started to cut out. The depth on both sides was less than a foot. As the boat drifted to a stop we checked the anchor locker and fortunately found the anchor was attached to chain, so we let out about 40 feet and came to a standstill.

We were out of gas.

We got on the VHF radio that was on the boat, and soon Vessel Assist appeared with two 5-gallon jerry jugs full of diesel. We paid them after dumping the fuel into the tanks and then got our first lesson in bleeding the fuel system. It would not be my last! Every boat has a different system, but luckily this one was fairly straight forward.

Once the motor was started we continued into Driscoll Marine for the survey. As it turned out there were no real surprises on the survey. The boat was truly in good shape. Not only that, but the seller was so happy I paid the full price he opened his garage and gave us a whole bunch of spare sails and gear that he was going to sell at a marine swap meet, but because I had not haggled, he threw them into the deal. On top of that he also left all the pots and pans, dishes, tools and spares that were on the boat. She was truly ready to sail!

While we were in the yard I hired a painter to come and put the new name on the boat. She would be known as Predator. I always liked those romantic names, and the movie Predator had just come out.

When the survey was over we headed over to my friend Tony's Harbor West Fuel Dock. We filled up and spent the night tied up behind the dock. Then it was an 11-hour tight sail to Catalina Island and Two Harbors, which has always been my home away from home. We had checked the anchor chain while hauled out and found there was 250 feet of chain to a 65-lb. CQR. That would be sufficient for where we'd be anchoring.

The boat handled well and sailed at about 55° off the wind at it's tightest, which was normal for a full-keeled boat.

A couple of days in Two Harbors and then we were off to King Harbor across the channel. Now the problem was, I gave up the mooring to Rich when he bought Lost Soul, so I didn't have a place to tie up. When we got in I asked the owner of the fuel dock if I could spend the night and he said okay.

As I had no place to keep Predator in King Harbor I spent a lot of time sailing over to Catalina. It was only a 4-hour sail, and once there, anchored in Two harbors it was like cruising. The only way to get there is by your own boat or the twice-a-day Catalina Ferry, but most people who took the ferry got off in Avalon which was 20 miles to the east. Two Harbors was still a sleepy little place with one store, one restaurant and two bars.

Two Harbors had been a military outpost

during the Civil War around the mid 1860s, and
was used extensively for shooting western movies
in the '20s and '30s. In fact there is a very large
herd of buffalo that are still there from those days.
They roamed free back then on the west end of the
island. William Wrigley bought the island in 1919
and there is still a Wrigley Ranch located in the
middle of the island. But the Isthmus, as the Two
Harbors area is also known, is operated by the
Catalina Conservancy which was created by the

*SV Predator
1981 Formosa 51 aft
cockpit*

Wrigley Family in 1972. There are photos of all the major movie stars from the '30s, '40s and '50s hanging on the walls of the bar, café and dinning room as it was a perfect way to get away from the crowds of Hollywood in a very short time. It is also where Natalie Wood drowned in 1981.

So this was my second home, until my personal world started to fall apart in 1986.

> Chapter 28 <
The World as I Knew It Comes
to an End and a New Life Begins

By then I owned Biker Lifestyle and Tattoo Magazines, both of which I had created from my old "FTW Newsmagazine" and "Chopper Guide" which I bought from McMullen Publishing. I was still a partner on Hermosa High, but didn't put in much time there anymore.

In July of 1986 Edmund Meese, at the time the Attorney General of the United States under President Ronald Reagan, sent a letter and list of over 100 magazine titles to the major magazine distribution companies that managed magazine distribution to 15-20,000 retail magazine outlets. In this letter he told them they "could be found liable for distributing pornography " if they handled any of the magazines on that list. The list of over 100 titles included Playboy, Penthouse and Hustler, as well as Easyriders, Biker and Tattoo.

Within 3 weeks I lost everything. I had two issues that were on sale when the letter went out. They were pulled from the shelves. I had an issue of each that had just finished printing at the printers. I also had an issue of each already in the distribution lineup, as these were all monthly titles. Each issue cost approximately $50-60,000 to print. I lost over $300,000 in a matter of less than a month.

I was broke. In fact, I was beyond broke. I was decimated.

My old friend, Joe Teresi, owner of Easyriders, called me up to see how I was doing. After a couple of meetings over a sushi lunch we made a deal. He would assume the debt and take over the titles. He had enough cash-flow from his other titles to carry it thru this disaster, and was part of the coalition to get Meese to retract his letter.

I couldn't argue with that, as my only other option would have been bankruptcy.

And so, all of a sudden I found myself free to do anything I wanted! The boat was paid for and I didn't have to put any time in at the head shop, as my partner, Daniel Herrera and his wife Casey, were handling that. For the next year or so I just sailed to Catalina and the Channel Islands a lot, and up and down the California coast.

Then this little girl, Tania Aebi went and screwed up my life.

Back then, everyone who was a cruiser read Cruising World. It was the bible and when it would hit the docks all would become quiet as people caught up on things. In every issue there was a story about this little teenage girl sailing around the world by herself. I was enthralled. I waited for each issue and couldn't wait to read how she was doing. It's kind of weird, but about 15 years later we would become best of friends and sail together all over the world.

Reading how this "mere girl" (she is probably grating over me using those words!) faced the day to day challenges made me want to get out there on a long ocean voyage. I was just looking for an excuse.

Then, in about 1988 one of my best friends, "Billy Jack" Withers, ended a little stay at Camp Fed where he had been killing time after a small

Bob at the helm of Predator

indiscretion concerning something that had been found in his possession. Being one of my best friends and having never sailed anywhere, I figured this just might be a good time to go out and have an adventure.

At the time I was dating a tall and statuesque blonde named Gina. Also, my son Bobby, 18 years old at the time, was visiting me from Texas and said he wanted to go too. I sold my half of a small house we had behind the head shop to my partner, and once we had enough cash we took off. The plan was to sail to Mexico, and then cut across to Hawaii.

It was a true fun adventure. We made the usual stops as we sailed down the Baja, and spent a little extra time in Cabo San Lucas visiting my friend at Latitude 22 (now known as the Roadhouse), Mike Grazenitch.

And then we headed further south. We made

Bob & Gina horsing around on the deck of Predator

a quick stop at Isla Isabela, and then went into Puerto Vallarta for a week or so. While there we heard about a new marina they had started to develop over in Nuevo Vallarta, a few miles up the coast. They had dredged a channel and even put in some slips.

There was no hotel up yet, as it was under construction, so we pulled in and found plenty of room for the boat right at the dock. This was years before they developed Paradise Village Marina across the way. There wasn't much available where we were staying, but it was free, so soon there was a full contingent of cruisers enjoying being tied to a dock and even tapping into the electricity.

Where we tied Predator up was soon known as "The Formosa Dock."

There were two other Formosa 51's that had tied up at the same dock. One was a cruiser, the

Talk about coincidence! Three Formosa 51's in a row!

other belonged to a lady that lived there in Nuevo Vallarta. It was a great site!

Every morning there would be a radio net from Puerto Vallarta that we would all listen in to. One morning I decided we needed to have a marine swap meet on the dock, and announced for folks to bring what they didn't need to see who was there that did need it. Some of the locals showed up too. My favorite was the lady that brought a big batch of fresh home-made tamales. They were two for 50 cents and to die for. We bought her whole selection for the boat the first thing in the morning, and she was back in a few hours with dozens more.

The swap meet was a raging success. People got rid of some of the things they didn't need, and as it turned out, the locals needed a lot of it.

Oh, yeah, kind of a funny thing happened while we were there. Liking to keep my boat in as nice shape as I can, I felt it was time to put on a coat or two of varnish. But my crew was revolting. No, not THAT way revolting, I mean they revolted against my plan to varnish. Amid weeping and wailing of, "it's too hot," and 'I don't wanna," I gave in.

There was a local kid there we'd met at the swap meet, Carlos. He was about 15 years old, large for his age, and he kept asking me if I had anything for him to do. I saw him sitting over on the seawall and called to him. I asked him if he knew how to varnish. He said he didn't, but he'd like to learn.

For the next couple of days I showed him how to rough the surface with the green Teflon pads and then wipe it down with a little solvent, and then how to keep a wet-edge while putting the varnish on. He was a fast learner. The first day the two of us did the cap rail. At the end of the day he'd done such a good job I asked him to come back the next day and work on some of the other external brightwork. He learned how to adjust using enough thinner to keep the varnish at the right consistency in the heat of the day. He learned how to repair cracks, and by the end of the following day Predator shined like a new boat.

While we went to Puerto Vallarta for the next day I had him polish the paint on the hull. When we got home I could see it shine even in the dark of the night.

The best thing about this story is this: Almost 20 years later I sailed in on Lost Soul II to the Paradise Village Marina where my friend, Dick Markie, was now Marina Manager. It is located just on the other side of the entrance channel from where we had tied up so many years earlier. As I walked down the dock a Mexican gentleman called my name.

"Hey Bob," he said, "When did you come in?"

I looked but didn't recognize the man. By then he had caught up with me, along with his companion that was walking with him. His

English was perfect and I was trying to figure out where he knew me from. Then he handed me his card. He owned the boat maintenance business that worked out of the harbor.

"You don't remember me?" he asked a little hurt, "I am Carlos. You taught me how to varnish many ears ago. Now it is what I do." He then turned to his companion, a good looking young man. "This is my son Miguel. He works with me now." His son was 18. Carlos then told me that when I left he kept varnishing boats that would come in. Then he learned mechanics, helping some cruisers fix their boats, and then electronics. He was running a full-service maintenance business.

I have to tell you, I was humbled by how well he had done for himself, the 15-year-old kid from the docks, now with a son of his own.

But, once again, I have digressed!

Predator in Las Hades

We stayed a few more days at the dock and then we sailed south to one of my favorite places, Las Hades. Ever since we were there on Stone Witch I wanted to go back. We had the time, so we headed south.

The sail down was fast & easy. We pulled in and spent a week lounging by the pool, swimming, nd just plain enjoying the decadence of the cruising lifestyle.

After a week we made our way back up to Nuevo Vallarta, to get set for our Pacific Voyage.

My original plan had been to sail back up to Cabo San Lucas and leave from there, but looking at a chart I figured we could just depart from Nuevo Vallarta and sail almost due west.

A very rare photo indeed. BB with no beard.

The day we left it was a beautiful sunrise. The sea stretched out in front of us and the wind was right where we wanted it. The first morning at sea Billy Jack and I decided to shave our beards off. We figured it would be at least two weeks or more before we hit land, so no one would see us but us. I had had my beard for about 20 years at that time, and Billy Jack had his about 10. So we both went below and cut off our beards.

I really look stupid without a beard. There are those who think I also look stupid with a beard, but without one even I tend to agree with them. We took a couple photos so we could remember why we wore beards, and sailed on.

The good weather lasted for about 2 days. Then we started to get a little weather. We didn't have a single-sideband radio, and our VHF was pretty much useless that far out. So we hunkered down and fought the headwinds and seas.

After another day we had been knocked down to less than 3-4 knots and couldn't steer anywhere near our course. It was very uncomfortable as the boat hobby-horsed something terrible with the head-on seas. That's something Formosas and other full keel boats are pretty much known to do. And to top it all off, my son Bobby had been practicing for the Olympic hurling team. He was hurling everything from his stomach a couple to three times a day.

He was not a happy camper.

I kept telling him all would be okay after the third day. As it turned out, this was not quite so. After three days he was about as sick as he could be, and I was starting to worry he might get dehydrated as he couldn't even hold down water.

So we turned back.

In the previous 5 days we had made a little

over 100 miles. We made it back to Mexico in
1 day! Sailing downwind rocks in a storm! It is
exhilarating! We couldn't believe how fast we
made it in.

As soon as we hit the docks Bobby asked me
to buy him a plane ticket back to Texas where he
lived. I felt bad that the trip hadn't worked out, but
he was insistent, so I acquiesced.

As it turned out, he found what it was he
liked to do when he got back to Texas. In the next
5 years he had five grandchildren for me!

Now the crew was down to three of us. Gina,
Billy Jack and me.

I decided that the trip to Hawaii was not in
the cards. Billy had enjoyed the sail down the
coast of Mexico, but was looking forward to
getting back "up the hill."

We sailed north as far as Mazatlan, where
we had a couple friends who would be coming
in to sail up the hill with us. One was my friend
Curt Albro, who was an avid boater who had just
moved over from the Dark Side. He was a power
boater who'd just sold his powerboat and bought
a 41-foot sailboat he'd named Here's the Deal. It
was a good name as he's a car dealer.

The other crew was Kevin Ryan who I'd met
just before sailing to Hawaii the previous time.
He'd wanted to crew with us then, but we couldn't
get it together. As it turned out, having him as
crew would lead to a very long friendship and
business relationship. Years later he would open

Outbound Marine in Dana Point, which is now one of the most well respected boat repair services in the area!

We pulled into Mazatlan Harbor once again; the home of the finless-brown and corn-backed lump trout. Here I have to make an admission. Those were terms that Kevin created off the cuff when he looked over the side and saw the effluent drifting past. I stole those names from him and have used them shamelessly hundreds of times since! Thanks Kevin!

We'd planned on leaving the next morning early, but around 11:00 p.m. a wind came up and our anchor was slipping. It seems that the bottom was covered with finless-brown and corn-backed lump trout and our anchor was slipping in that crap (I guess literally!) drifting us toward the seawall. We decided it was time to leave. We hoisted the scum-covered anchor and headed out

Latitue 22 - The Roadhouse, our home away from home.

of the breakwater for open (clean!) water.

The winds coming down from the Sea of Cortez were about as good as we could ask for, so Curt and I stayed up the rest of the night and well into dawn. It was one of the few perfect sails I can recall. Light seas, light winds, but enough to fill the sails and keep us moving at 6-7 knots. It was perfect! It's a 215 mile sail from Mazatlan to Cabo San Lucas and this sail was great all the way across. Even in the evenings, with a light wind blowing and not a cloud in the sky, it was like being far at sea. It was peaceful and serene.

While in Cabo we pretty much lived at Latitude 22 The Roadhouse. Mike had moved into a great new loaction, right behind Costco. What better location for a cruiser?

After a week in Cabo restocking and waiting for the winds to be right, we headed out and around Cabo Falso. Curt had flown home as he had to get back to work, but we still had Kevin, Billy Jack and Gina. We were, indeed, lucky this trip. The winds were not strong so we tacked up the coast, stopping along the way inside Bahia Magdelena, Santa Maria and then we sailed into San Juanico. This is a very small village, but a nice protected anchorage against the fairly steady northern trades.

After a good night's sleep in San Juanico, at dawn we started to pull anchor and head out. There was some seaweed blocking our path so I just upped the RPMs a little and told Billy Jack to go forward and make sure there were no rocks. As the bowsprit glided over the seaweed it woke a humpback whale that had been dozing in the seaweed. The huge animal woke with a start and "snorted" strongly through his spout. It happened to be just as Billy Jack was directly over the spout standing on the end of the bowsprit. Whale snot is not a very easy thing to wipe off. Poor Billy Jack smelled like whale snot until the sun came out and it was warm enough to take a sun-shower. I don't know who was more upset, Billy Jack or the whale!

As we approached Bahia Tortuga the wind started to increase, and a few miles out we had to start the motor and motor-sail tight into the wind to try and make it in. Bahia Tortuga, or Turtle Bay, is one of the best protected anchorages on the Baja. We made it in just before sunset. (See Rule #1)

Anchored in the bay were two of the sleekest boats I had ever seen. As it turned out they were delivering these two boats from Italy. It was the Il Moro de Venezia team.

The next day on the net we heard that the windy weather was supposed to hang around for a few days so we announced on the radio we would host a cruisers' gathering on Predator. There were only a few boats there and it sounded like fun.

And it was. The next day about a dozen people came over to Predator for the party; everyone in the harbor except the people off one small boat that was anchored a hundred feet or so away. I asked Billy Jack to take the dinghy over and invite them, as they had not been on the net. In a few minutes he came back with two people. It seems they had lost their dinghy and their VHF didn't work. They were just finishing up an 11-year circumnavigation.

Oh, yeah, and they hated each other! They couldn't wait to get back to the U.S. so they could get a divorce. They had to sell the boat to get it, but both agreed that would be just fine with them. As soon as they hit the deck she went below and he went up on the forward deck to talk to the people there.

One highlight of the party for me was when the delivery skipper from Il Moro invited me to go aboard. I had never even seen an America's Cup boat, and this one was famous! Everything about the boat was built for speed. Once inside the slight lapping of the waves echoed loudly, as there was no lining, just the hull and the equipment inside. There was a nav station at the bottom of the steps, but the rest of the boat was wide open. I asked him where they slept and he showed me how you pulled the pipe-berths down, and slept on the hard canvas surface, if indeed you could sleep at all with the noise. Oh, and they had sailed non-stop from Italy to the Panama Canal, and non-stop from the canal to Bahia Tortuga where they decided to pull in due to the heavy weather.

I was impressed!

A couple days later the Il Moro told us their weather forecaster had said the next day would be good for heading north, so at first light we headed north. We made a non-stop run into San Diego Bay.

Now I have to tell you, I had no plans to go or do anything. I'd been working on a book while I was cruising, but once we were in San Diego I was at a loss. Tony at the fuel dock said we could stay on the back side of the fuel dock if we could get in there, so get in we did.

Oh, yeah. One of life's little embarrassing moments came back to haunt me when we pulled into the fuel dock. Once we'd tied up I went into Tony's office with him, telling him about the trip and such. Pretty soon we heard a whole bunch of laughter outside. It was side-splitting laughter, so we went out to investigate.

You see, I used to do a newsletter to a couple hundred of my friends. To do this I would compose the letter on my computer and send it to my friend, Glenn Stewart. He had a business and his secretary would make a hundred or so photocopies of the letter (usually a couple pages long) and put them into envelopes and mail them. Well, we had also sent our rolls of film to him. When he picked them up he found the photos of me without my beard. It looked so funny that they made a couple hundred copies and included them in the newsletter! A lot of people in San Diego would come to Harbor Island West Fuel Dock to read the newsletter updates. And Tony thought it was so funny that he posted it on the bulletin board with my beardless photo. I, of course, did not see a lot of humor in it.

Well, maybe a little!

> Chapter 29 <
Doing a Book, a Movie and
Another Offer I Can't Refuse!

I decided that I liked the waterfront in San Diego. So I made arrangements for a slip in Harbor Island West, which was the marina that Tony's fuel dock serviced. I got a great slip out on the end of the 300 dock, and we settled into the San Diego boating lifestyle. Billy Jack got a job at the fuel dock. Gina got a job at Club Marina Bar where they advertised "Semi-Live Music." I started working on a book I'd been writing at the time, "Emerald Bay." It was a sequel to my first novel, "A Brotherhood of Outlaws."

So one night we are at a bar on Shelter island and we run into a bunch of like-minded partiers. Before the night was out we had invited them to the boat for a day sail. As it turned out, one of the guys was "Bear" Paul, and he was the Key Grip on a bunch of movies, and as a matter of fact, was working on a new movie at the time, "K9" with Jim Belushi.

While we were out sailing he said they needed some more grips and asked if I wanted to come work on the movie. Duh! Yeah! You bet! I'd worked on a couple TV shows when I was in Hollywierd and thought they were fun. And so, the next day I found myself parked in my 1974 Red Eldorado convertible on a side-street while they filmed Jim Belushi and the dog in his 1965 Mustang swinging out of control in a drift towards my car! They took the shot at least 6 times, and each time I thought my car would be wiped out, but it was never touched.

After that I started working as a grip. We worked for a week or so during daylight hours, and then they went to shooting at night. It was fun and I had a ball. I got paid too!

One of the most fun things was when we were shooting this scene at a small private landing strip near the Mexico border. The scene was supposed to be Belushi meeting "the bad guys" who swoop in on a helicopter to trade his girl for the keys to a truck filled with drugs.

So it was about midnight when they were ready and had the shot lined up. But first they had to have the armorer check the guns. They were all loaded with blanks, but they had to make sure they would all fire. So the armorer, his crew, and a few of us grips grabbed a gun, and at a given signal we fired into a much of bushes. All of a sudden the bushes came alive! People started running out of the bushes saying, "No dispares! No dispares! Nos

Vamos! A rough translation means "Don't shoot. Don't shoot. We are leaving!"

It was pretty funny to all of us, but I don't think those who were in the bushes enjoyed it quite as much!

In all I really enjoyed working on that movie. And it gave me time to finish Emerald Bay.

Eventually, Gina moved off the boat and so did Billy Jack. But we would still get together and go out for day sails whenever we could. The early arrivals for the America's Cup were practicing and they were fun to watch.

One Sunday, a perfect "Chamber of Commerce" day, we went out for a day sail. The weather out on the bay was perfect. This huge bay was completely surrounded by land so there was no swell. There was a good stiff breeze and Predator loved it there.

After being out for a few hours we were heading back into Harbor Island. As we approached Tom Ham's Lighthouse, which sits on the tip of Harbor Island, we got ready to drop the sails. Now I am kind of a nut when it comes to trying to look good coming in from a sail. Billy and Gina had sailed with me enough to know the routine. So as we sailed toward the island I had Billy bring down the staysail. Once it was down, just before we'd hit the 5 knot speed limit sign, I would fire the engine, drop it into gear, and at the same time I would release the headsail sheet while Billy let go the halyard. At the same time Gina would release the main halyard so the main would drop into it's "Dutchman" system on top of the mast, while I did the same to the mizzen.

All the sails dropped at one time and then Billy and Gina put on the black sail covers. As we passed Tom Ham's Lighthouse we were looking good!

In fact we may have been looking too good.

As soon as we tied up in our slip a man was walking down the dock towards us. He stopped by the boat.

"Whose boat is this?" he asked.

"It's mine," I boasted.

You wanna sell it?" He asked.

"Everything's got a price," I responded.

"How much?" he asked.

I thought for a quick minute. I didn't really want to sell it, but...

"$195,000.00" I said, knowing no one would pay that for the boat.

"Be okay if I bring my client down?"

"Sure. Why not? Just let him know we just came in from sailing so it's not completely ship-shape. Bring him on."

A few minutes later they came aboard. The buyer never said a word. He walked thru the boat, looking at everything, for about 5 minutes. Then he went on deck. Looked in the aft deck box, felt the sail covers, and then walked off the boat without a word.

The broker stuttered something and left with

him.

Oh well, I figured. Nothing ventured, nothing gained. We went below and started getting ready to make some dinner. About 5 minutes later there was a knock on the hull. I went topside, and it was the broker.

"My client wants to know if you'd take $175,000."

All of a sudden I really did not know what to say. So I asked him, "Do you have a deposit to make that offer?"

He said, "No, but I have been showing him boats all weekend. He flew in from Alaska Friday and this is the boat he was looking for. He is serious and he owns a few fishing boats up there, so I don't think money is a problem."

I thought for a minute. "Make it $185,000 and we can do it."

He smiled. "Be right back."

And he was. The man wanted it, for $185,000, and he wanted to do the survey Monday. This was Sunday.

"I can't do it that fast," I told him. "I live aboard and it will take me a week to make new plans."

He said he was sure that was okay and gave me his card.

"Call me in the morning and I will let you know if I have a deposit check or not." Then he continued. "I know I will. He wants this boat."

So did I, but I'd bought it for $110,000 just

a year earlier, and to make a profit like that on a boat was unheard of. I had to do it.

The next day I called, and the broker said that he did, indeed, have the 10% deposit, and the man wanted to haul it out for survey the following Monday. I had a week to figure out what to do.

He also said the man did not want anything that was on the boat. None of the tools, dishes, pots, pans or even spares. Not even the dinghy. He wanted all of those things removed.

I had met a couple cruisers, Mike and Jack,who I had helped survey their boat a couple of weeks earlier. Mike was a woman. She was a large woman, standing about 6 feet tall and weighing in at about 180 pounds. Mike was a slender man of small stature. He stood about 5' 5" and weighed about 150. They were perfect together. I had never seen a more compatible couple.

What brings this up is, they had just bought a boat and needed a bunch of stuff. I made a deal with them to give them the pots, pans and dishes, if they would help me put on a dock sale for the next 6 days. They agreed and they plastered fliers all over Harbor Island and Shelter Island, as well as at the local yacht clubs. The flier had the boat's slip number and a partial list of the stuff I had to get rid of.

Meanwhile I needed another boat. And quite frankly, I had made enough on this one so I wouldn't have to be so careful.

> Chapter 30 <
My First New Boat

Walking up the dock, at the top of the dock I saw a Catalina 42. It was a 1990 model, all brand new and pretty. I walked into the brokerage. No one was in a hurry to approach me. I guess it was the fact that I was in scrungee cutoff Levis, a black Harley-Davidson T-shirt with the sleeves cut off and the neck cut out. It might also have been the tattoos. Who knows? But I wandered around the boat yard looking at this big, shiny, beautiful new boat.

Finally someone must have drawn the short straw. He walked over and stood there.

"How much?" I asked, pointing at the boat.

"$110,00.00," he answered politely.

"Is that sail away? And if so, what comes with it."

He walked me to a desk inside, and you could see a couple of the other salesmen smirk. Fuck 'em. This was going to be fun!

The salesman stated to warm up a little and

showed me what the standard equipment was.

"But," I said, "I thought I saw a self-furling headsail and some other extras on it."

"Oh," he said, "Yes. That one is one we are putting into the San Diego Boat Show next month. It has a few extras that are not standard at that price.

"Okay, if you will sell it to me for $110,000, as is, I'll take it."

He sat there just looking at me. Then I noticed him look around the showroom and saw the smirks on the other salesmen's faces.

"You know what?" He said, "I think we can do that. How would you be financing it?"

I said jokingly, "Would you take cash with two forms of ID?"

"I'll be right back," he said and walked off to the brokers office.

A few minutes later he was back. He had a smile on his face. "If you'll let us put it in the show we will do that."

"Well, there's a problem with that. You see, I just sold my boat out on the docks and they take delivery next Monday. I need a boat this week so I can move my stuff aboard, because I liveaboard."

I waited as this sunk in. Once again he walked to the brokers door. I could see he was fighting hard for this. I think it meant more to him to make the other salesman look foolish than the actual sale!

Once again he was back. "Okay, you've got it.

I told the owner I'd take a cut in my commission and he agreed to it."

"How much of a cut?" I asked.

"Not much. Just enough to charter one of these to put in the boat show. We don't have another new one, but we do have one in charter."

"Okay, I'll make you a deal, dinner on me at The Lighthouse!"

And I was now the owner of a brand new 1990 Catalina 42. Once again I had to go for a romantic name. I named her Assailant!

Oh, yeah, there was another silver lining to the black cloud that was the selling of my boat. At the docks that week and that weekend I raised almost $20,000 selling crap off my boat! No, really! It was amazing how much junk we accumulated on the boat. I was hesitant to sell my tools, but honestly, they were pretty rusty and all, and what could go wrong on a brand new boat, right?

Yes, once again it is time to go back to Rule #3. Never ever ask, "What could go wrong?" You will find out soon enough.

But when the docks had cleared I'd sold everything I had on the boat including the dinghy and motor. It was too large for the Catalina 42, so I replaced my 12-foot RIB with the 25hp Honda outboard with a 10-foot Apex with a 15hp Honda outboard.

I had finished the book "Emerald Bay" and the movie K9 was long-time over. I decided it was

time to head back up to Redondo and see what
kind of trouble I could get into there.

It had always been a minimum of 15 hours to
Catalina from San Diego. The trip from Catalina
to San Diego was about 10 hours, as the winds
were always behind you, but sailing uphill to
Catalina you could count on direct headwinds.
So I planned for a 15-hour trip. I figured if I took
off at 5:00 a.m. I would get in around 10:00 p.m.
Since I knew the harbor, Rule #1 did not come
into play.

I have a place I anchor in Two Harbors,
actually between 4th of July Cove and Cherry
Cove, where no one else anchors. It's 108 feet
deep and people figure it's too deep for a good
anchorage. But after 20 years of hanging out there

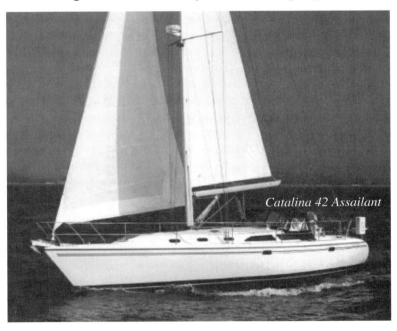

Catalina 42 Assailant

I knew the bottom better than most men know their wife's bottom. Where I would drop my 300 feet of chain with oversized 65-lb. Bruce hook would hold great. If the wind blew on shore the boat would drift over about 45 feet of water, and there was no way I was going to drag 300 feet of 3/8" chain and a Bruce anchor up that grade. And if the winds were to reverse, I would be in the lee of the island and the bottom stayed at 100-110 feet for a half mile behind me. I couldn't drag that far even if I tried with my motor in reverse! It was perfect for me.

So at 5:00 a.m. I untied the dock lines on my brand new, shiny Catalina 42 Assailant and headed out the mouth of San Diego, past Point Loma, and hoisted the sails. As the sun came up I was well clear of land and single-handing made me feel like a real sailor again. I had put on an autopilot, so I was able to kick back and relax.

The wind was, as expected, tight on the nose, so I cut a little closer to land on a port tack. The boat was unbelievable. After over 10 years of sailing Taiwan Turkeys (full-keeled boats built in China) this boat felt as if it was sailing right into the wind. I tightened sail and was able to hold 30°, which was about 20° better than I had ever been able to sail. The course I was holding was just a bit off the course to Dana Point. I figured I would tack a couple miles prior to there.

As it turned out, and as the day progressed, the winds allowed me to tack early and I made it as far as Avalon, about 20 miles shy of my goal, by 5:00 p.m. It was only 20 more miles to two Harbors. I was stoked. I'd never really sailed on a boat that had that kind of performance.

It was about 8:30 p.m. when I dropped my hook. The sun had just set and I dropped my dinghy in the water (I had it tied on the foredeck where I hoisted it with my halyard) and headed into Doug's Harbor Reef for a Buffalo burger and a couple of Buffalo Milks.

For those of you unfamiliar with a Buffalo Milk, I can tell you, it has everything in it but the kitchen sink, and it tastes like a chocolate soda. Here's the recipe, which was a well kept secret for many, many years.

1 oz vodka

1 oz Kahlua® coffee liqueur

1 oz creme de bananas

1 1/2 oz dark creme de cacao

1 - 2 oz milk

This is all topped off with some whipped cream and a cherry. You drink a couple of those and find yourself brushing the floor off your shoulder.

That night I found the only thing wrong with my new boat. As I dinghied out to the boat I didn't know which one was mine. Ya see, for all of my sailing life until then I could tell my boat by its silhouette. The bowsprit, the double masts, and just the bulk of her and I knew I was home. The Catalina 42 was sleek, low, and in the dark looked like all the other boats.

Oh, I did find it all right, but that was the first thing I found to be disappointed about.

After a couple days I was ready to sail back to my home port. My friend Curt had arranged for a temporary slip right down the dock from his boat.

Before dawn, about 5:00 a.m., I hauled the anchor, turned on the running lights, and headed out past Bird Rock and Ship Rock. These were two landmarks sailors have used for years to find Two Harbors. Just as I was passing Ship Rock, which is about 1 mile out from the anchorage, I smelled smoke. Now, if there is one thing you do not ever want to smell on a boat it is the smell of something burning, unless it's the coffee!

But this was not coffee. It had the acrid smell of an electrical fire.

I had just raised the main and was getting used to my first furling headsail when the odor hit me.

I cleated off the sheet to the headsail and checked the autopilot. I decided to kill the engine in case that was in some way the cause of the fire. Then I headed down below. The smell was much stronger (I had hoped I was smelling something from ashore). I opened the port aft cabin door and was blinded by smoke. I could barely see the glow of a fire at the very rear of the cabin.

The battery switch was near the companionway so I reached down and shut it off. I grabbed the fire extinguisher that was by the companionway, took a deep breath, and went into the cabin blasting in front of me with the extinguisher. The glow died and I rushed back out the door to get a breath. By then the smoke had filled the cabin and I started choking.

I ran up the companionway stairs to get some clean air. Then I noticed there was smoke coming out of the port-side lazerette. I walked back and opened the lazerette only to find another small orange glow of fire.

I'd had a fire extinguisher installed on the steering pedestal, so I grabbed it. As the smoke cleared I could see where the fire was still burning and I hit it with the extinguisher. The glow died.

The sails seemed to be handling the boat just fine even with the autopilot off from when I had shut off the electrical power. I went below and opened all the ports and hatches. I'd left the lazerette hatch propped open. The smoke cleared and I could see that the fire had started in an electrical wire loom, right where it passed from the steering pedestal into the lazerette. The harness had burned about 2 feet and into the aft of the rear cabin.

I decided to sail the rest of the way in, just in case, and about an hour before entering King Harbor I called Sluggo, a friend of mine who lived on the same dock I was coming into, to see if he was on his boat. He was.

When I sailed into King Harbor it was like coming home. I made the turn down the main channel and dropped the headsail as I did. I was moving at about 4 knots. When I hit the channel I needed to turn into, I would be going directly into the wind, but was blanketed by the hotel that sits on the little island we were tucked in behind. I drifted down to about 2 knots and then turned it sharp into the slip. Sluggo was there to help me pull in.

The first thing I did was take Sluggo up to the bar where Jody was working (she was new and had no idea that years later we would be married!) and bought him a drink or two for helping me get into the slip without scratching my new boat. Then I called Catalina Yachts and got one of the biggest surprises of my life.

The receptionist answered and I told her I'd just bought a Catalina 42 and had a fire on it. She politely asked me to hold on a moment. In less than a minute I heard, "This is Frank Butler, how can I help you?"

Okay, I might have been a newbie to Catalinas, but everyone knew who Frank Butler was. He was a legend in California (and most other sailing areas) as the man that introduced affordable sailboats and got more people into sailing than anyone else before or since. I told him what happened. He listened, asked one or two questions and then said, "Don't worry about it. We will make the boat like new again. I will have two men at your boat tomorrow morning. Will that work for you?"

"Uh, yeah sure," was about all I could get out.

I have to tell you, I was impressed. I had half expected to get a runaround like, "Well, we didn't sell you the boat, so you gotta call the broker," and that would be followed by, "We didn't commission the boat, so you gotta call Acme" from the broker.

But no. The boss man himself took the call immediately. Most of the conversation for the rest of the day at the bar was about how that went down.

And sure enough, at 8:30 the next morning 3, not 2, men showed up. One was Gerry Douglas, the boat's designer and chief engineer. At that time I had no idea who he was. In the years since we have become friends. He looked the boat over for about 20 minutes and then came to me before heading for the factory in Grenada Hills. He told me what had happened was that there was a 20-gauge wire tied into a 12-gauge wiring harness. It was for the compass light. It had been pinched when the compass was installed and had shorted out when I turned the running lights on.

He then went on to explain that they would replace the wiring harness, refinish the whole aft cabin, supply a new cushion so there would be no fire smell, and they would have it done in a day.

Once again, pure astonishment. The next day I got a call from Frank Butler, the man himself! He told me he wanted me to know they had made a construction change on the technical specs for the boat, and from now on all Catalinas would have a fuse installed on the compass light electrical lead, so what happened to my boat would never happen again.

About 23 years later, in 2013, I would have the honor of roasting Frank Butler when he was inducted into the Sailing Hall of Fame and was recognized by the industry for introducing more people to sailing than any other single individual. You can bet I told that story to everyone in the sailing industry at the ceremony held in Annapolis, MD.

But back to life aboard Assailant. Life back in the marina was going easy. In fact, too easy. There was not enough teak to keep me happy; just a little teak around the door and the door slats themselves. I used to love varnishing and how it

Bob & Frank Butler at Frank's industion to the Sailing Hall of fame in 2013

224

made the boat look. Assailant looked great sitting there, and I have to admit she was so easy to sail she almost sailed herself. But she didn't offer much of a challenge.

As I am sure some of you are aware, idle hands are the Devil's playthings. And so it was with me. I was bored and I didn't care for being bored. So I had to find some trouble to get into.

The first thing I did was to open a small jewelry store opposite a new movie theater that opened in Hermosa Beach. It didn't take much of an investment, and I had my partner Daniel and another partner, Jimmy Hess, who had been doing my books for the past few years. The store was named Zzyzyx. I figured we couldn't be the first one in the phone book. Who wants to name a store AAA Aardvark? So we might as well be the last.

We took turns working the store and I made one of the best deals I ever made on the rent. You see, they had just built the new shopping center called the Hermosa Pavilion, and it was not real popular, as it had 5 levels of parking below the building so it was not like normal California Shopping Malls with miles of parking. BUT, the theater was popular as it had 5 screens.

And we got the location right across from the theater.

The deal I made with them was, they gave us $10,000 for "build out" which means to put in walls, carpets and lights, and then we'd pay rent on a 5-year lease. But since the mall was empty

I got them to add a small condition... Our rent wouldn't start until the center was at least 50% full.

Long story short, it never got to 50% filled. And we did great being across from the theater. In fact, this is where I came up with Nautical Gold Creations. We had a jeweler who would come in twice a week to do repairs for us. He was good. In fact, he was so good that here, 30 years later, we still work together!

But back then I had lost a bracelet while drifting down the river in Tenecatita, Mexico. I called the one company I knew of that made a cable-chain bracelet like I wanted, but they wanted way too much money. So I asked Hector, our jeweler, if he could make a chain bracelet. He told me to bring in a few links so he could look at it.

Well, cable chain is huge. It's what they use on large ships. So I was off to the salvage yards of Long Beach, where I found 3 links of cable chain. Each link weighed 50 pounds! The three links weighed 150 pounds. I loaded it into my car and drove back to the store. I managed to get it over my shoulder and dropped it in front of his jewelry repair station.

"Like that." I said.

He looked at the links.

"How big would you want the links?" he asked.

"About like this," I said, holding my fingers a little over ½" apart.

He picked up some calipers off his table and measured between my fingers.

"I'll make a wax and see what it would weigh."

The next day he showed me a small wax link of a cable-chain.

"Like this?" He asked?

I looked at it. "Yup, that looks perfect."

He took out a tape measure and measured my wrist. Then he did some calculations, and dropped the wax chain link on a scale.

"14 or 18 karat?" He asked.

"14," said I.

"I can make one for you for about $1800," he said.

That was about half what the other guy wanted.

"Really? How long would it take?"

As it turned out it took him a couple days. The end product, which I still wear today, was the first of a hundred styles including Turks head rings, shackle earrings, four different sizes of solid cable anchor chain for bracelets and necklaces along with close to 100 nautical themed gold items. Oh, and the price he quoted me was retail! My price turned out to be much less.

And then, I was contacted by the National Maritime Historical Society asking me to run a business card-size ad to support the society. I took a photo of the bracelet, which he had made with a working shackle closure, and put the small ad in offering the bracelet for $1800. We sold two.

I started advertising in Sail, Yachting and Cruising World. All of a sudden I was in the nautical jewelry business. Who knew it was that easy?!

But back to boating.

Being a man of the single persuasion, I was doing a lot of dating and my favorite "tactic" was to meet a waitress or bartender, and invite them to sail over to Catalina when they got off. As they would get off at 2:00-3:00 a.m., it made for a perfect romantic sail to the island, arriving at sunup and, well... let's just say life was good.

And that was how I met my wife, Jody.

Jody worked at the Portofino Yacht Club. It wasn't a real yacht club, but as the Portofino Hotel and Marina was the only tenant on the small island in the marina, they called their bar a yacht club. The bar was where everyone who was a regular in the marina hung out. They had happy hour, and tenants got a discount from that, so it wasn't that expensive and they even had free pu pus for when we'd get the munchies.

Jody's first impression when I walked into her bar for the first time was, "I'd sure hate to run into that guy at night in an alley!"

Over the next year I would go day sailing just about every day. Whoever went sailing with me, we'd go up to the bar after the sail. It was like a private club.

One of Jody's first memories of me was when

she came in to work the early shift on a Sunday. My boat was in the slip right below the windows of the second story bar. The night before I had met a young lady, and as things sometimes happen, she ended up on my boat that night after a heavy day of imbibing. Alcohol and bad judgment combine sometimes to create a perfect moment! I guess the fact that it was warm out had something to do with it, but it seems we ended up naked, asleep in the cockpit of Assailant. The girl must have woke early, and being embarrassed (she was getting married the following week I found out later!), she departed, leaving me in the nude al fresco in the cockpit. Jody was polite enough to come down and wake me so I could go inside and get dressed.

That was in 1990. We were married in 1996. I guess she liked what she saw, huh?

And speaking of such things, my friend Curt, who I have mentioned a couple times here, started dating the bar manager at the Yacht Club, Jill Holiday. They "started dating" right after the three of us went out for a day sail on Assailant. She was the daughter of a very old friend of mine. They were married a couple years before Jody and I, and were the Best Man and Maid of Honor at our wedding aboard the Lost Soul in 1996.

But once again I have altered course from the subject of this book, Sailing, sailboats, and why it doesn't take a rocket surgeon to enjoy it!.

In less than a year I started to ache for the traditional sailing vessel. Assailant was easy to sail, fast and everything any sane man would want in a boat. But I never was very sane. I missed the look of the bowsprit, the aft cabin with windows across the stern. And I missed the teak. The way my boat would look after she was polished and varnished, would bring a lump to my throat.

The Catalina, although easy to maintain and easy to sail, just didn't get my juices flowing. And so it was I put her up for sale and started looking for my "dream boat."

> Chapter 31 <
Finding My Soul

I guess, looking back, I was starting to mature. I hate to admit it, but all of a sudden staying out drinking wasn't as much fun. I even reached a point where I tired of the dating scene. I know. I was probably just off my meds, but it happened.

At the time I was dating Melody, a beautiful woman with rich black hair, a build men die for, and she was the VP of a multi-national company so she actually had a job. Not just a job, but she made more than I did! AND she had a condo right on the beach.

Melody and I decided it was time to settle down and get married. We became engaged. Her job had her on the road a lot, so I had plenty of time to sail. But I was on the lookout for "the perfect boat."

Now here I gotta say, a man's idea of a perfect boat and a woman's can differ quite a bit. The first boat I looked at and fell in love with

was a three-masted steel schooner named Golden
Dawn. I wanted it, bad. But the owner wanted a
little more than I could get together.

I still owned a vacant lot by the beach in
Hermosa Beach, so I offered to trade that as part
of the payment and we almost had a deal! But at
the time, in 1990, real estate in California was
on a roller coaster and it was moving down as we
tried to put the deal together, so I lost out on that
one. As it turned out, 5 years later when I pulled
into Niuatoputapo, Tonga, I sailed Lost Soul right
over the top of her. The man who'd ended up
buying her took her cruising and it sank going thru
the pass.

I found two traditional Formosa-built boats
in Southern California that were along the line of
what I was looking for, a Formosa 51 in Channel
Islands and in Ventura Harbor, about 10 miles up
the coast, was a Formosa 56. Melody and I made
appointments to see them both on a Saturday and
drove up.

The Formosa 51 was a dream boat. It had
been used by the owner to party on and they never
even put a stove in it. Below decks it was brand
new. The motor had less than 150 hours on it. The
boat was just 5 years old, but above decks looked
like it had never been washed. Other than that, it
was perfect. And even more perfect, it was listed
at $99,000 and the broker said $80,000 would buy
the boat.

I said I wanted it. Melody said no. We'd made

an appointment and it would be impolite to stand the guy up.

The drive to Ventura Harbor was filled with me telling her how perfect that boat was. In a week I could have the teak sanded and a few coats of varnish on it, and the hull could be polished out.. etc.

When we got to Ventura Harbor we found the dock where the other boat was tied up. Standing on the sidewalk looking down, it looked like a total disaster. It was obvious she had been ridden hard and put away wet! There was junk all over the deck, and the poly windows were scratched and faded so bad you could hardly see thru them. I was sure Melody would hate it. I hated it if only because of the name painted on her stern. Fair Weather! I'm sorry, but I was used to the more romantic names, Rogue, Outlaw, Lost Soul, Predator and Assailant. Fair Weather just didn't do it for me.

We found the broker and boarded the boat. The rigging was old and frayed, the varnish cracked and half gone. The aft deck was piled with tools, and wires were strewn all over, including sticking out from under the mizzen mast.

We stepped down into the crowded storm room; crowded with junk, and Melody started to step into the boat. She stopped.

I thought, "Oh boy, now I can go and get the other boat."

She turned to me. "This is it," was all she

said.

I was flabbergasted! I couldn't believe that she would want this piece of crap. It was obvious the boat had been worn out. I couldn't even imagine what it would take to put her into sailing shape.

Melody stepped aside and I walked into my next boat.

She was right. This was not a boat, it was a sailing ship. Below decks she was set up for long distance cruising. She had a raised inside steering station as well as the one on the aft of the center cockpit. There were teak handrails everywhere, so no matter how far the boat was heeled you could hold on. The galley was tucked along one side of the companionway, which had steps, not a ladder. There was a landing as you walked in, and down from there on the starboard was a real navigation station, with plenty of places for books and charts.

Yes, the first boat would have been easy to turn into a cruising boat, and this one would be a lot of work. But this was a ship.

I don't need to go thru the negotiations. Suffice it to say, they asked $135,000. I offered $100,000 and we settled on $110,000.

A week later I was sailing south to King Harbor under a collection of raggedy old sails on the boat that was to become Lost Soul.

The story behind the boat was part of its charm. It had been built for the black sheep of a Colorado farm family. He'd sailed it around the world and then abandoned it in Papeete on its second voyage.

The owner had a friend, Steven King (no, not THAT Steven king), who was very much into sailing. I'd met him in Hawaii when we were there years ago on the first Lost Soul. He was living on a beautiful schooner. We were actually docked next to each other in 1984 when Wyland was painting a mural next to the Kaiser Hospital in Ala Wai. Many an afternoon we wasted sipping on a cold drink, watching Wyland work his magic. Wyland would come over every once in awhile for a cold beer. It was a great memory.

Ah, but once again I am off-point.

The owner had asked Steve if he would sail the boat back from Papeete. He agreed. When he got as far as Hawaii he anchored it in Kalihi Lagoon under the airport. And there it sat for three years. Meanwhile, people moved onto it. They took a couple of the hand carved teak doors off and hocked them. They sold the sails off her. Then she started to go down until her motor was underwater.

In the meantime, poor Steve King sailed into San Francisco Bay on his schooner and was promptly arrested and sent to jail for importing smokable substances. When Steve got out he had lost everything. Then he remembered the boat he'd left in Kalihi. He contacted his buddy, the owner, and found out it was still sitting in Hawaii. He made a deal with the guy to sail it back to

California, fix it up, and they would split what they got for it. By the time we'd found the boat they had already replaced the diesel, rewired the 12 volt, and were about halfway thru rewiring the 110.

One of the funniest things to happen was as we were pulling into the haul out facility at King Harbor Marine. As we were coming down the channel heading for the travel-lift, Steve pulled back on the throttle so he could put the boat in neutral. As it turned out, the throttle stopped working and we were motoring at the dock at about 6 knots. Steve hit the kill button, but the engine didn't die. He had me grab the wheel and ran below, opened the engine room, manually down-throttled and manually threw the boat into reverse.

He hollered up at us, "Tell me when I should kill it!"

As soon as we'd slowed to about a knot I told him to go ahead. We drifted right into the travel-lift dock, sweet as you please!

The next two days were a fuzzy haze as we did the survey and finalized the deal. The survey was really a joke, and the surveyors list was long.

Rule #9. When you pay for a survey, get your moneys worth!

It took the surveyor the full day, but he managed to find just about everything that was wrong with the boat. It was a very long list.

On Monday morning everyone was gone. I

walked into the King Harbor Marine yard early
and stood looking up at the behemoth of a vessel I
now owned. No one was there yet, and I walked up
the temporary stairway that led to the deck. Once
on deck I looked around, and then sat down on
an overturned bucket on the aft deck. Everywhere
I looked I saw a lot of work that had to be done.
And then there was the varnish, and polishing out
the hull. Tearing out the antiquated electronics. It
still had a vacuum tube radar set!

Then there were the sails. The rigging.
Everything. I sat there completely overwhelmed,
thinking I had just made the biggest mistake of
my life and wishing I had bought that pretty little
Formosa 51.

I guess I'd been sitting there about 15 minutes
and had absolutely no idea of how to start. I saw
the ladder move, and pretty soon Curtis' head
came into view. He didn't say anything, just pulled
up a box of crap that was nearby and turned it to
sit on it.

After a minute or so he said, "So where you
gonna start?"

I shook my head. "I have no fucking idea. I
think I may have bitten off more than I can chew
with this one."

We sat there in silence for another minute or
two. They were very long minutes.

Then Curt stood up and turned to me, "Okay,
let's go down to the corner by Home Depot and
see how many workers we can pick up. That's as

good a start as any."

"Yeah, I guess so," I said, and then I knew the first step.

> Chapter 32 <
Living The Dream

A year later, with the Lost Soul II looking like a million bucks, I was ready to do some "serious" cruising. I was tired of dreaming and wanted to start living. One morning Melody and I were having coffee with Jim, the Harbor Master, and he asked me when I was going to give up my liveaboard rights.

I looked at him like he was nuts. "I'm not," I exclaimed. "Why would I do that?"

"Because you're getting married aren't you?" he asked innocently.

It was then I noticed the look on Melody's face.

Jim finished his coffee in a gulp and mumbled, "Well, I gotta go. "I'll talk to you later." He was out the door faster than I think I'd ever seen him move before.

There was no way Melody could live aboard. She was an executive and her closets were bigger than my whole boat. And besides, she had a beautiful condo right on the beach.

And there was no way I was about to give up my lifestyle.

We were in a quandary. And it was one that we could see no way out of.

We remained good friends and still saw each other, but it was soon common knowledge that we would not be getting married.

And I very much wanted to go on an adventure!

Over the next few months I started dating again, and then one weekend I was dating a young girl named Adriana who was a very good friend of Jody's. At that time Adriana was planning to go sailing with me, and I was busy planning an extended voyage to Suverov Island in the Northern Cook Islands. I'd found a book by an Australian named Tom Neal (not the one who has written for Cruising World) called "An Island to One's Self." It was about a man who fought for years to find a way to this small atoll in the middle of the South Pacific, and finally did it in the mid fifties. The book was compelling and all I could think of was, I wanted to read it again, anchored at that island. The only way to get there was to sail there on your own boat!

I once again entered the mental paradise known as planning a voyage. It started with a trip to southwest instruments down in San Pedro, and charts were ordered, looked over and drooled on.

My copy of Earl Hinz Landfalls in Paradise

*Lost Soul II sailing
in Bonduras Bay,
Mexico*

got dog-eared more & more, as I wandered
the islands of paradise in my mind, and could
almmost see myself standing at the wheel as we
pulled into nuku Hiva, Hiva Oa and Papeete.

Looking at the photos of Bora-Bora nearly
drove me nuts. I wanted to be there, but more than
that, I wanted to live the life of Captain Adam
Troy from the TV show Adventures in Paradise.

One weekend Jody joined me and Adrianna
on a sail to Catalina Island. At the end of the
weekend we sailed back to Redondo, dropped
off Adrianna, and Jody and I sailed back. Within
another week Adrianna decided she was going to
stay in Redondo, and Jody had gone to Melody
and asked her if it was okay if she sailed with me
to the South Pacific. Melody said it was fine with
her, and today Jody, Melody and I are best friends.
She has sailed with us all over the world. But she
still has her condo, and she still has a closet bigger
than any boat I have ever owned.

It's just about this point where my book
"Letters from the Lost Soul" starts. It was written
and serialized in Latitudes & Attitudes Magazine
from 1997 thru 1999, and then published by
Sheridan House in hard cover in 2000. It has since
been reprinted 3 times.

And so I will leave you with this thought.
Let's call it Rule #10. Don't dream your life, live
your dream.

Bob's 10 Rules For Cruisers

Rule #1
Never enter a strange anchorage at night.

Rule #2
Never assume.

Rule #3
Never ask what could go wrong. It will.

Rule #4
Prepare for the worst, hope for the best.

Rule #5
Make sure everyone aboard knows the rules.

Rule #6
Be sure to know who you take on as crew.

Rule #7
Always have paper charts aboard when cruising.

Rule #8
Any boat you own should make you feel comfortable.

Rule #9
When you pay for a survey, get your money's worth.

Rule #10
Don't dream your life, live your dream!

About The Author

Bob, Jody & Fred aboard Lost Soul

Adventure has been a way of life for Bob Bitchin since the early sixties, when his name was coined by the comedy team of Cheech and Chong. He worked as a traveling companion and bodyguard for famous motorcycle daredevil Evil Knievel, promoted motorcycle shows, and created Biker Magazine and Tattoo Magazine in the 70's and early 80's. He also worked as editor of many of the motorcycle magazines of that era, and wrote for other publications as diverse as Forbes, Penthouse and New Look. During that time he rode his motorcycles across the country over 30 times, and around Europe as well. He was the founding president of the Motorcycle Press Association in 1978 and co-founder of ABATE National.

For almost thirty years he lived aboard sailboats and cruised most of the Pacific and Central America since the early seventies

In 1986 he sold his magazines and started sailing full time. He bought the staysail ketch Lost

Soul in 1990, and he and his wife Jody sailed the world until 1996.

In 1996 he created Latitudes & Attitudes Magazine. In the 15 years of its existence it became one of the largest and most authoritative publications on sailing and world cruising.

In 2011 he sold the magazine with plans of retiring, however it turned out the buyers were a "bit less than honest" and they never paid him, emptied the bank accounts and disappeared to Central America.

That is when the miracle occurred.

After losing everything, at the age of 69, as he was in bankruptcy, a group of Latitudes & Attitudes readers came forward and formed a "Founders Circle" for a new magazine. They hired Bob to run it.

The new magazine, Cruising Outpost, became the premier cruising magazine of the genre. It was soon the biggest selling marine title at chain stores like Barnes & Nobel and West Marine.

Bob now divides his time between Publishing Cruising Outpost, world cruising, doing seminars on sailing and writing.

Oh, yeah, and riding his Harley!

This is his 8th book.

Bob and his wife Jody now live in Berry Creek, California between the north and middle forks of the Feather River.

Bob has two children, 6 grandchildren and 3 great-grandchildren.

Biker to Sailor

Other Books By Bob Bitchin
(All Bob Bitchin books are available at BobBitchin.com,
CrusingOutpost.com and Amazon.com)

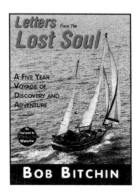

Letters From The Lost Soul
By Bob Bitchin
This is the story of the voyage that created Latitudes & Attitudes Magazine and the television series of the same name. It is also responsible for creating Cruising Outpost Magazine.

Excerpt from Letter From The Lost Soul

The crew for this leg consisted of one large, tattooed captain, one well-endowed first mate (Jody), two deck slaves (Canadian college students Luke and Joel), and, of course, our newest kidnapped, Kari. We finally made it out of Vavau and headed north to Niuitopatupo Island, which is the northernmost island in the Tonga chain. On the way out of Vava'u, another seam let go in our new mainsail. This was almost a record, as the last tear happened leaving Bora Bora, at two hours out. This one lasted two and a half hours after we'd gotten it fixed in Niafu by the sail-maker from the yacht Jacaranda. We sailed the rest of the way to Niuitopatupo under a reefed sail, which was slow going, since we only had 10 knots of wind. That was just part of the fun. About halfway (90 miles), we noticed our bilge pump going off excessively. A quick check showed we were taking on water from a one-inch hole in our main engine exhaust system. I went to shut down the through hull only to learn that the gate valve was stuck. Oh joy.

I tried to shove a rag in the one-inch hole. Kinda like the little Dutch boy and the dike. It then became a three-inch hole. It seems that the galvanized elbow had rotted through from the inside. Now we were taking on water faster than a Jewish mother takes on guilt. In fact, more water than our 3,000-gph bilge pump could handle. No problem. I turned on our secondary emergency bilge pump. This could almost handle it, but just to be safe I figured I'd check the hand bilge.

Oops. No handle. Forgot to get one before I left home. Oh well, no problem, we still have the three-inch-high pressure emergency gas-powered bilge pump.

Er, except we loaned our last gas to a man in a panga who was out of fuel as we were leaving Vava'u. So we had no gas. The next 10 hours were spent in deep prayer, as I turned on the engine to lessen the water leaking in.

With the engine on it was just the exhaust water coming in (and filling the boat with exhaust so we all had to stay outside). If I shut the engine down the water came in a three-inch gush. Too much for the bilge pumps. Just so you don't worry too much, if it had become a problem we could have shut down the engine and plugged the exhaust from the outside, and sailed in with no problems. I just like to make it sound hairy for literary purposes (honest mom!).

We made it into Niuitopatupo and spent the day repairing torn sails, fixing exhaust elbows, (ain't West epoxy great stuff?), and kicking back.

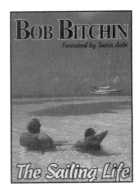

The Sailing Life
By Bob Bitchin
This is a collection of insights into why people love the sailing and cruising lifestyle. Each one has an example of a lesson learned at sea.

Excerpt from From The Sailing Life

You've just pulled out of Gibraltar and headed around the southern tip, on your way to Ibiza, Spain. Your significant other is down below, and you're on watch. You stand holding the wheel watching the ships that squeeze through the bottleneck at the straights of Gibraltar, and wonder, "How many centuries have men felt this wonder?" In front of you is all the history you have read about, and you are about to discover it for yourself, at your own pace. An unsurpassed feeling of anticipation fills you.

• • • • •

The boat is going to right itself. The fifty-foot wave that just broke over you slammed you down a bit, but the boat took it, and is popping back up just like it's supposed to. You tighten the main sheet to where it should be, and check the reef lines. Everything is okay. You hollar down to the crew below that it's over, and then it hits you.

What if the wave had been bigger? What if the stays hadn't held? The mast could have broken! Or the keel bolts broken off! What then? The boat would have capsized. And what if the safety harness hadn't kept you in place when the wave hit, or, God forbid, what if you hadn't put it on? Look behind you. There is nothing back there, and you wouldn't have been missed for an hour or so. At least until the next person was going to come on watch. Can you imagine what that would be like? Treading water and watching the boat sail off without you?

It always seems to come after the worst is over. During the storms, the ordeals, or the tight reef entrances. But when it's over. That's when it hits.   Fear! Gut wrenching fear.

• • • • •

Your arrival in the Marquesas was supposed to be after 22 days, and here you are, pulling in after just 18 days. The storms that pushed you were hell. The rain seemed to find every place that leaked on the boat, and you were really getting pretty tired of trying to find a dry spot in the bunk.

Beans and cold stew had been your meal more nights than you might have hoped, and the

auto-pilot going out at the halfway point didn't
help much either.

But there, in front of you. Nuku Hiva! Look
at the spires. The harbor looks like heaven. More
colors of blue in the water and more colors of
green on the hills than you even imagined, and
you are here on your own boat.

You've done it! As you look at the small tear
in the mainsail, a feeling sweeps over you. You
prepared your boat to the best of your ability.
You planned for the storms, and the fuses that
went out, and the wet weather.

And now you are pulling into your first South
Pacific paradise under your own power. The
storms, the seas, the 2,800 miles behind you seem
like nothing. You can't help but smile, as you
wave to a passing cruiser who is heading out of
the channel.

"Yeah!" You say to yourself, almost aloud.
"Yeah, I made it. The boat made it. The crew
made it. And only a handful of people on Earth
can ever say they have accomplished such a feat.

The feeling is so strong you almost feel a
chill.

Pride. The pride of conquering unknown
peril to accomplish a goal.

• • • • •

The squall hit late at night. Your wife was on
watch, and she hesitated to wake you, but the sails
had to be reefed, and it takes two.

Since she's on watch she feels it's her place

to go out and handle the reeflines, so you turn the boat into the wind to let the sail luff, and watch as she ties each line. All the miles behind you, and she still has the same feeling for the boat. And for the lifestyle.

She finishes tying the lines and gives the high-sign. Everything is okay. You turn down wind to fill the sails, and adjust the sheet line. The rain is coming down hard now, and as you look up you see her walking between the house and the lifelines.

It had been warm on her watch, so she was wearing a bathing suit. Then the rain hit so she has a poncho on. You look up from the winch and she's standing there, rain running down her face, with the biggest grin you've ever seen. Your heart melts.

Love. Pure and simple.

• • • • •

There is no other lifestyle on this water-planet that can evoke such feelings, such depth of emotion, as cruising. The challenges that meet you only make them stronger. Being in charge of your own destiny becomes a way of life, and most cruisers find, if they ever stop cruising they can't return to their old lifestyle. But then again, who the hell would want too?

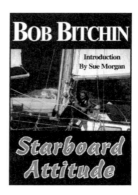

Starboard Attitude

By Bob Bitchin

This is the sequel to The Sailing life. Once again, taking small vignettes from life at sea, and bringing forth a lesson to be learned.

Excerpt from From Starboard Attitude

Why is it, when I look up at my flag halyard and see the Jolly Roger flying proud in the wind, I want to smile? What's up with that?

Every day we hear of ships off the coast of Somalia being boarded by pirates. I find myself taking offence at the use of that term. They aren't pirates. They are thieves, terrorists or hijackers, but they are not pirates.

No, to me, pirates are a romantic notion of a lifestyle best portrayed by Captain Jack Sparrow in Pirates of the Caribbean! A bunch of seafaring gypsies that lead a life of adventure.

The fact that real pirates stole, killed, raped and murdered has no place in my dream world. To me they were adventurers. It's very much like the image of the Old West. The heroes we have from Dodge City and the cattle drives on the Chisholm Trail were, for the most part, murderers and bad guys. But after a couple hundred years, they have become something else.

Yes, I know pirates were not nice people. But the fact remains, and I can't explain why, when I see another boat with a skull & crossbones flying from the yardarm, I feel a kinship. It's kind of like meeting a kindred spirit; someone who looks at life the same way I do.

It's funny, because when I meet someone with no sense of humor (I really try my best to avoid people like that, but as you know, sometimes it's not that easy!), I find it difficult to justify my admiration for thieves, cutthroats and murderers.

But none-the-less, when I look up and see the Jolly Roger smiling from my flag halyard, it makes me smile. It makes me feel good, and when I am lucky enough to be around a few hundred people of like mind, well, it just plain feels like home.

I have been enjoying the cruising lifestyle for over 30 years, and in that time I don't think I have ever really met a pirate. Oh, I've met some thieves, mostly in urban areas of the world. One must keep an eye out to protect their goods. In Papeete I remember standing watch to protect our dinghies from being stolen. But they weren't pirates. They were people who didn't have anything and looked at cruisers as rich people with boats.

When we were sailing to Europe in the mid 1990s we were told to avoid visiting Naples, as there were a lot of thefts going on. As it turned out, we had to anchor off a suburb of Naples awaiting parts for a busted generator. It was one of the best stops of the voyage and nothing happened.

When anchored off the Nicaragua/Honduras border at Media Luna Reef, we were approached by a suspicious vessel late at night, with no lights on. They were probably thieves. Standing watch with a sawed off 12 gauge seemed to change their attitude, and we had no trouble. I don't know if they were thieves, but they definitely were not pirates! As a matter of fact, in the 30 years I've been sailing I have not only never met a pirate, I've never met anyone who has met one.

The earliest documented instances of piracy are the exploits of the Sea Peoples who threatened the Aegean and Mediterranean in the 13th century BC. The Illyrians and Tyrrhenians were known as pirates, as well as Greeks and Romans.

But the real age of pirates came much later. In medieval Europe the Vikings from Scandinavia raided from about 783 to 1066. Vikings even attacked coasts of North Africa and Italy, the Baltic Sea and rivers of Eastern Europe as far as the Black Sea and Persia.

Muslim pirates terrorized the Mediterranean

Sea. In 846 Muslim raiders sacked Rome and damaged the Vatican.

The classic era of piracy in the Caribbean extends from around 1560 up until the mid 1720s. The period during which pirates were most successful was from 1700 until the 1730s. It was here the classic view of the pirate was born.

And here is where I get my best ammo against the nay-sayers who denigrate pirates! It was the pirate brotherhood who invented democracy (kinda!). Pirates were some of the first to use a system of checks and balances similar to the one used by the present-day United States and many other countries. The first record of such a government aboard a pirate ship dates to the 1600s, a full century before the United States' and France's adoption of democracy in 1789.

So I guess that gives me a slight edge when talking to those weirdos who say, "Why do you have a pirate flag flying? Pirates are nasty people!"

I can point with pride at my Jolly Roger and say, "I support democracy! And it was the pirate captains that first practiced it!"

Aaaargh!

A Brotherhood of Outlaws

By Bob Bitchin

A Brotherhood of Outlaws is a novel, and has been called the most relevant look at the outlaw bikers culture in the 70's & 80's era ever written. It was initially sold as hard cover by Bentree house Publishing, and is currently in it's 6th printing. It was translated into German and was a best-seller in Germany.

Excerpt from A Brotherhood of Outlaws

I glanced up from my speedometer and saw the broadcaster eyeballing down on me. Hell, I hope the pack is centered. I would hate to go to all this horsecrap and lose out on any of the exposure. My fatbob Harley was running as good as it had ever run and the feel of the vibrating power came right through the handlebars. All I could think about was the snake behind me. I looked into my rearview mirror and once again my heart beat a little harder.

Jesus H. Christ, there is no better feeling in the world than leading 30,000 bikes down the

road. Unless it might be leading 40,000 bikes
down the road.

Just before we passed under the bridge I
looked back up at the broadcaster. I had seen him
before, at the park. He was kind of a little guy,
but he seemed to know the score. I like him. Most
of the newsmen that were sent to cover this protest were cocky new, because, after all, it was just
a bunch of bikers sniveling about their rights
being stepped on.

Makelray was different. Like he knew I had
plans for this group. I don't know how, but he
knew.

Passing under the bridge made us sound
even louder. The thunder roared and it was beautiful. I glanced next to me at Rom and he had this
big shit-eating grin on his face. I guess the sound
was getting to him too.

Rom and I had been through a lot in the last
two years together, and this was going to be the
payoff. I reached into my cutoff jacket and felt for
my security. It was my 357 Magnum. The heft
alone made me feel good.

We turned off the Golden State and onto the
Pasadena freeway, toward the civic center. Hell I
hope those cops got the blockades up and the traffic re-routed. If they don't, I would just as soon
take this pack through downtown Los Angeles. I
was sick and tired of the bureaucracy bullshit that
had been going on for the last few days and right
now I really didn't give a rat's ass if they were

ready or not. We got a point to make and brother are we going to make it.

We turned off the Pasadena and onto the Hollywood freeway. Just one more mile to go. As we dropped into the hollow under some bridges the echoing sounds of the pack came back to me and I was ready for anything. I could ride like this forever.

Our off ramp loomed ahead and I slowed the pack from 45 to 30 miles and hour. No use dumping some sidewalk commando and listening to the government turkeys harp on unsafe riding or other such horsecock. This day was set aside for bikers and dammit, that's whose day it is. Period.

As we approached the civic center I could see all the police there. A quick glance up showed a couple of helicopters in the silver sky. I could see this was going to be a well-chaperoned event.

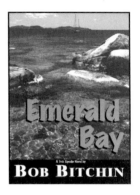

Emerald Bay

By Bob Bitchin

A novel featuring Treb Lincoln and others from A Brotherhood Of Outlaws. But now Treb is living on a Sailboat, and an explosion in Emerald Bay in Catalina starts he and his friends on an adventure that ends up leading them to Central America and right into the middle of a CIA partnership with the drug cartels.

Excerpt from Emerald Bay

The San Pedro Channel was pretty calm and there were four- to five-foot swells spaced very far apart. It made the 120-foot boat roll a little, but not enough to be uncomfortable. She got up to her cruising speed of 22 knots and settled in, while the partiers did their damnedest to drink the bar dry.

On the aft deck, a bunch of girls were dancing to the music being piped over the speakers, and much to the enjoyment of the guests and crew, a couple of them started to strip. It was normal for them to do since most of them worked at Shipwreck Joey's back in LA, which was one of the nicer titty flop bars.

Matt was the bouncer at Joey's, and he was acting as master of ceremonies and wardrobe assistant. As the girls would take off a piece of clothing, they'd hand it to him. He would smile and then throw it over the side.

A trail of clothes followed the boat almost all the way to Catalina.

On the bow, Treb, Dick, and Rom passed a bottle of Southern Comfort and a joint.

"Well Bro, you gonna miss this kind of life or what?" Rom asked.

"Why should I miss it?"

Dick looked at him hard.

"In case you didn't notice, you're getting old and you just got married."

"Who you calling old?" Treb smiled. "I ain't no older than you, and I can kick your ass just like always."

Dick started laughing and passed the joint. Treb saying he could kick his ass had always been a standing joke. When it came to fighting, there was no one who could beat Dick.

Dick Bondano and Treb had met 13 years earlier in a bar fight in Las Vegas. Treb had come into this small bar just off the strip while he was riding across country.

About five or six very large truckers had decided they wanted to see if this big biker could handle a whipping, so they jumped him.

Dick had been sitting at the bar nursing a

three-day drunk after getting fired from his job, and he relished the idea of a real kickass brawl. He watched as three truckers took turns on the big man, and soon he could see the biker really didn't need much help, but he wanted in, so he jumped in with both feet.

At six feet and 180 pounds, Dick wasn't all that large, but his Hawaiian ancestry gave him a mean look, and he was wiry as hell. Besides that, he had been raised in a martial arts family. His father, his grandfather, and all of his uncles were Masters in Filipino Kali, the ancient art of weaponry. Dick had been trained since childhood in Kali and Jeet Kun Do. He had worked as an instructor at Bruce Lee's old school, the Jeet Kun Do Academy, and until Vietnam, martial arts were his life.

After all the killing in Nam, he decided to opt for a little less violent occupation and ended up in Las Vegas working as a guard at a chemical company.

As he waded into the fight beside the large biker on that day 13 years ago, his life changed.

Ever since then, they had been inseparable friends. They rode around the country for awhile and then settled in the South Bay area of Los Angeles. Treb had opened a gym and Dick had gone back into martial arts with a vengeance. Now, at 38 years of age, he owned a martial arts school in Torrance and was a coach for boxers and wrestlers as well as teaching his real life love, kickboxing. Whenever things would start to get to him, he'd enter the ring as a sparring partner and let off steam.

It had always been a joke between Treb and Dick that Treb could kick his ass. They both knew it wasn't true and laughed about it.

"Ok," Dick laughed," so when did Karen say you'd have to sell the bike?"

Treb laughed and swung at him haphazardly. When Dick caught his hand they tumbled to the deck, rolling and laughing like a couple of kids.

"Hey, come on you guys!" Rom laughed and he started to pour Southern Comfort over the two on the floor.

Dick's hand flashed out of the jumble and pulled Rom's feet out from under him. In a few seconds there was 750 pounds of biker in a pile with Southern Comfort adding to the sticky mess.

King Harbor

By Bob Bitchin

A Treb Lincoln novel that follows Treb and his friends from the docks of King Harbor in Redondo Beach, California to a remote island in the Pacific where they end up saving the lives of hundreds of islanders.

Excerpt from King Harbor

As I climbed aboard Lost Soul I remembered why I hate boats! No matter how you baby and pamper them, they never seem to get enough of your attention. They just seem to find ways to remind you that they are the important one in the relationship. When I was younger I often wondered why it was they were referred to as she. After a few years of living aboard and crossing a few oceans, I started to understand the similarities. Like a woman, they seem to get jealous if you spend any time with another boat, and if you don't come home just one night they will make your life miserable.

It was a typical King Harbor morning in

King Harbor Southern California. The sun was shining, the seagulls were soaring overhead, and bikini clad cuties were rolling along on wheels on the road in front of the marina. After spending the previous couple weeks delivering a new Catalina 42 sloop up to the Bay area, I was real glad to be back where the sun shines. Four hundred miles uphill is never a good sail, but this delivery had gone pretty much as planned.

I was delivering a new Catalina 42 from Marina Del Rey up to San Francisco for a broker I did a lot of deliveries for. After leaving Del Rey I sailed up past the Channel Islands in perfect weather. I sailed on a tight reach up to Point Dume, and then made a few tacks up past the Islands. I pulled into the Cojo anchorage and sat there waiting for a good weather report to make it around Point Conception. I timed my arrival at Point Conception for just before dawn, when the northeast tradewinds were the lowest, and once around that notorious landmark I'd just hugged the coast for the rest of the voyage.

It's a long stretch of beautiful coastline as you make your way up, sailing past Big Sur and Monterey. It's beautiful, but dangerous, and with absolutely no place to pull in if you hit any trouble. It's about as rugged as a coastline can be.

I found myself enjoying the trip, watching as I paralleled Highway One. In my previous life, when I was riding motorcycles, this was my favorite getaway; throw a sleeping bag on the bike and ride up Highway One. It doesn't get any better, and I relived a few of the trips as I sailed passed Lime Kiln Cove and Big Sur.

After dropping off the boat at the dock in San Francisco, I picked up my paycheck from the broker who'd hired me to deliver the boat and grabbed a taxi to the airport. I couldn't wait to get back home. Of course, on my return, my baby made it known to me that I had better stop staying out for weeks at a time. Being left by herself, she always seems to get a real attitude. The longer we've been together, the more attention she wants when I neglect her.

After this voyage up north, she was particularly displeased with me. "My baby" is my home, a 56-foot stays'l ketch I named Lost Soul. I'd saved her from the bottom when she was about to be scrapped.

After she'd gone around the world a couple times she'd been abandoned for a few years, and was in pretty sad shape when I found her. Since her shape pretty much matched my bank account, it seemed we were destined for each other.

Biker

By Bob Bitchin

This was the first book by BB, written in the late 70's as he rode around the country and the world writing for various motorcycle magazines. These are all true stories. If you are offended by sex, drugs or Rock & Roll you may want to pass on this one!

Excerpt from Biker

That evening I started looking for a hotel early, not wanting to be left out in the weather. After I tried three of them I gave up, and settled for a campground in Monte Carlo.

The folks who ran the campground were the epitome of the word assholes. They were ripping off folks left & right for 37 francs a night to camp motorcycles and only 20 for cars. Even so, there was no other place in Monte Carlo a biker could stay, so the campground was where I ended up.

That night I decided that Europe didn't really have much that I didn't have back in the good old US of A, and I made a mental note to start heading back to Frankfort for a plane ride home.

Once the Bitchin boogie fever hits me slow travel is all over. I aimed the bike out the gate of the campground at 6:30 in the morning, and by 11 AM I had crossed into Italy, ignoring the odd looks by the Gestapo at the border, headed north, away from the Mediterranean and up into the Italian Alps. I zig-zaged across the French border three or four times, and soon was crossing through the St Bernard Pass and into Switzerland.

When you cross into Switzerland there is a tunnel that was almost two kilometers long, and I really got a kick out of it, nut when I went over St Bernard Pass I found that there was a tunnel five kilometers long, and inside the temperature was a constant 30 degrees.

Since it was in the 80's outside I was riding in just my T-Shirt, and when I hit the tunnel I nearly froze my butt off.

All books by Bob Bitchin are available at BobBitchin.com, CruisingOutpost.com, Seafaring.com and Amazon. Most are also available as downloads.